Voices captures the inner dialogue in our heads and hearts that distract and deceive us, seeking to allure us away from Jesus. *Voices* winsomely offers life and freedom from Proverbs, helping us to see how God's wise voice is warning and inviting us to come to him, where true joy and everlasting love is experienced. *Voices* is a powerful discipleship resource to equip everyone in the church.

> **Robert Cheong**, Pastor of Care, Midtown,
> Sojourn Community Church, Louisville, Kentucky

Here's a book jam-packed with practical, biblical wisdom, brought right down to every day life in an easy-to-read style. The passion behind this series is that too many resources for growing Christians are parked in the wrong places: they don't deal with the pressures and fun of normal life. Andy has shone a spotlight on the life-changing truths of the book of Proverbs, made sense of them in the overall bible story, connected them to Jesus at the centre, and then parked them right where you live. Read it on your own, or with a friend or two, and you'll learn how to hear God's voice, today.

> **Chris Green**, Vicar, St James Muswell Hill, London
> Author of *Assemble the People Before Me: The Message of the Church*

VOICES

WHO DO I LISTEN TO?

ANDY PRIME
SERIES EDITOR MEZ MCCONNELL

CHRISTIAN
FOCUS

Scripture quotations are from *The Holy Bible: New International Version*®. NIV®. Copyright © 1973, 1978, 1984, 2000, by International Bible Society, www.ibs. org. All rights reserved worldwide.

Copyright © Andy Prime 2017

paperback ISBN 978-1-78191-912-5
epub ISBN 978-1-78191-927-9
mobi ISBN 978-1-78191-928-6

10 9 8 7 6 5 4 3 2 1

Published in 2017
by
Christian Focus Publications Ltd,
Geanies House, Fearn, Ross-shire,
IV20 1TW, Great Britain.

www.christianfocus.com

Cover and interior design:
Moose77.com

Printed and bound
by
Bell & Bain, Glasgow

All rights reserved. No part of this publication may be reproduced, stored in a retrieval system, or transmitted, in any form, by any means, electronic, mechanical, photocopying, recording or otherwise without the prior permission of the publisher or a licence permitting restricted copying. In the U.K. such licences are issued by the Copyright Licensing Agency, Saffron House, 6-10 Kirby Street, London, EC1 8TS www.cla.co.uk

CONTENTS

INTRODUCTION

My name's Andy Prime and I'm part of a team planting a church on a housing scheme in Edinburgh, Scotland. A scheme is what we call a socially disadvantaged and deprived neighbourhood in Scotland. Planting is hard work anywhere. But one of our struggles is that there are very few resources written for and applied to our context. There's not much out there for a new Christian from a community like mine to help them grow to maturity in Christ. The aim of this book is to help you hear the voice of your Heavenly Father amid the countless other voices demanding your attention. It aims to convince you that His voice is not just worth listening to, but that He is worthy of your love and your life. My hope is that this book will not only be useful for the new Christians from my community, but for those in similar communities around the world.

ANDY PRIME
Gracemount, Edinburgh

HOW TO USE THIS BOOK

The First Steps to Discipleship series will help equip those from an un-churched background take the first steps in following Jesus. We call this the 'pathway to service' as we believe that every Christian should be equipped to be of service to Christ and His church no matter what your background or life experience.

If you are a church leader doing ministry in hard places use these books as a tool to help grow those who are unfamiliar with the teachings of Jesus into new disciples. These books will equip them to grow in character, knowledge and action.

Or if you yourself are new to the Christian faith, still struggling to make sense of what a Christian is, or what the Bible actually says, then this is an easy to understand guide as you take your first steps as a follower of Jesus.

There are many ways to use these books.

- They could be used by an individual who simply reads through the content and works through the questions on their own.

- They could be used in a one-to-one setting, where two people read through the material before they meet and then discuss the questions together.

- They could be used in a group setting where a leader presents the material as a talk, stopping for group discussion throughout.

Your setting will determine how you best use this resource.

As you work through the studies you will come across the following symbols ...

Gary's Story – At the start of each chapter you'll meet Gary and hear something about his story and what's been going on in his life. We want you to take what we've been learning from the Bible and work out what difference it would make in Gary's life. So whenever you see this symbol you'll hear some more about Gary's story.

Illustration – Through real life examples and scenarios, these sections help us to understand the point that's being made.

STOP – When we hit an important or hard point we'll ask you to stop and spend some time thinking or chatting through what we've just learned. This might be answering some questions, or it might be hearing more of Gary's Story.

Read 3x – The Bible is God's word to us, and therefore it is the final word to us on everything we are to believe and how we are to behave. Therefore we want to read the Bible first, and we want to read it carefully. So whenever you see this symbol you are to read or listen to the Bible passage three times. If the person you're reading the Bible with feels comfortable, get them to read it at least once.

Memory Verse – At the end of each chapter we'll suggest a Bible verse for memorisation. We have found Bible memorisation to be really effective in our context. The verse (or verses) will be directly related to what we've covered in the chapter.

Summary – Also, at the end of each chapter we've included a short summary of the content of that chapter. If you're working your way through the book with another person, this might be useful to revisit when picking up from a previous week.

MEET GARY

The early years
Gary has always been one of the lads. Growing up on a notorious housing estate in England's northern town of Sunderland, his mother left home when he was just a toddler leaving his dad to raise him and his little sister. He still doesn't know why his mother left, he probably never will.

Gary didn't think much about work. Almost every man he knew used to work down the coal mine. That was never an option for Gary after the pits closed before he started High School. When the pits shut down he watched his dad's life slip away to alcoholism and gambling. Gary never had a real job but has made ends meet by cashing in his benefits cheque while also working from time to time at his mate's mechanic garage.

Life now
Now in his late thirties, Gary is still one of the lads. He lives on the council housing estate near his dad and sister. Most nights he plays football with his mates. He moved in with his long-term girlfriend and they are raising their teenage son. Gary is known on the estate as a man who is humorous, loves to party, and will do anything for you.

Everything changed for Gary when one of his best mates became a Christian. He couldn't believe it. He had never really met a Christian before but he couldn't deny that something real had happened to his friend. Gary had a ton of questions and patiently his friend worked with him until eventually he also gave his life to Christ and trusted in Him as his Saviour.

This is Gary's story...

WHAT'S THE POINT?

LIVING RIGHTLY IN GOD'S WORLD BEGINS WITH RELATING RIGHTLY TO GOD.

ONE:
WHERE DO I BEGIN?

GARY

Gary's been a Christian now for six months. He loves Jesus, but that feeling of being at war hasn't gone away. And now, as if living in the trenches wasn't enough, everybody seems to be telling him different things. His head's spinning. His pastor keeps pointing him to Jesus. But the problem is He's not the only voice.

His wife seems happy he's around more, but keeps nagging that he's not providing for her as well since he straightened up.

His dad's keeping his distance, but warning him not to take this religion stuff too seriously.

Some of his mates pat him on the back and tell him how well he's doing, but he gets the feeling they're waiting for him to fall.

A couple of the boys are always in his ear offering him an easy way back into the old easy lifestyle.

And then there's that one lad who loves the conspiracy theories and is certain the church has brainwashed him to control him.

Add to that the voices in his own head: Is this war really worth it?

Wasn't your old life way more satisfying than this?

Did you really leave all of this behind to feel like this?

You really think you belong here, and deserve this?

When he used to make decisions it felt like he had an angel on one shoulder and a devil on the other. Now it feels like there's about a hundred on each shoulder.

Who should he listen to?

 ILLUSTRATION

Remember when you were at school, and you and your mates walked into a classroom but instead of your normal teacher stood at the front, there was a supply-teacher standing there? Remember the thought that went through your mind?

'Today, we can get can away with anything.'
But imagine the next day, your normal teacher's still off, but instead of the supply-teacher, the headmaster's stood there. Now what goes through your mind?

'Today, we can get away with nothing.'
The point is that our relationship to someone always impacts our behaviour around them. It's not just true of pupils when a teacher walks in the room. It's true of you whether or not the person who walks in the room is...

> your brother
> your gran
> the police
> your dog
> someone you're attracted to
> your step-dad

How we relate to different people as they enter the room impacts what fills our thoughts and flows out in how we behave.

STOP

Q: Gary's got loads of voices in his head – his pastor, his partner, his dad, his friends. How might Gary's behaviour change depending on which one of them is in the room with him?

3X 'The proverbs of Solomon son of David, king of Israel.' **Proverbs 1:1**

Right off the bat we see that this is a book written by a man called Solomon who is the son of a King. We might be tempted to think he must have been a clever fella who's had his life together and had everything he ever wanted. So, maybe it's tempting to think, 'What can this guy have to teach a guy like Gary? He's living in a different world.'

But, don't be so quick to judge because when we jump into Solomon's story, we soon find out that he was a <u>normal guy</u> trying to make sense of life, and as <u>full of insecurities</u> as most of us. When he was about to take over from his dad as the King of Israel, he tried to wriggle out of it, and made his excuses to God saying, 'I am only a little child and I don't know how to carry out my duties.'

How can I be a king when I feel more like a dunce?

But in the end, he prays to God saying, 'Give me a discerning heart.'

In other words, 'God, give me wisdom.'

In **1 Kings 4:29-34** we read that God heard his prayer, and makes him the wisest man on the planet. He became so wise and smart that, eventually, people would travel the length of the planet to hear his wisdom. <u>If God can give Solomon wisdom and make him wise, He can give anyone wisdom</u> – **even Gary**, and make him wise. In fact, the book of Proverbs is the *Wise God*,

giving His foolish people a *wise king*,

that they might learn to *live wisely too*.

God gives it to Solomon, that he might pass it on to people like Gary.

The book of Proverbs is massively important for Gary and for all Christians. Why? After all, it's not the first book that would jump out at us from the Bible. I'm not sure it would make the top 10 of most important books to teach new Christians.

It's important because King Solomon points us to an even greater King, the greatest King

JESUS

In **Matthew 12:42** Jesus is referred to as someone far greater than Solomon. Therefore, as we read through this short book together we need to remember that it's not just ancient history that has nothing to do with us. The book of Proverbs is

the Wise God,

giving us

His foolish people

the wisest King,

that we might learn to live wisely.

STOP

Q: When Gary's feeling overwhelmed by all the voices in his head, how can he make sure that he gets this voice – the voice of God's wisdom – into his head?

3X '...for gaining wisdom and instruction; for understanding words of insight; for receiving instruction in prudent behaviour, doing what is right and just and fair; for giving prudence to those who are simple, knowledge and discretion to the young.' **Proverbs 1:2-4**

The first verse told us *who* wrote the book. These next verses tell us *why* he wrote it.

1. **This book is going to teach Gary how to <u>think</u>** (v. 2).

   <u>A Christian thinks very differently</u> from those around them.
   The world's wisdom and God's wisdom are <u>not</u> the same thing.

Gary's a new Christian, just getting to know this stuff. Becoming a Christian for him is no small thing but it is going to re-engage and re-do his entire thinking so that he *'loves the Lord his God with all his mind.'*

2. **This book is going to teach Gary how to <u>act</u>** (v. 3).

   <u>A Christian acts differently</u> from those around them.
   The world's morals and God's morals are <u>not</u> the same thing.

One of the important things about Christian behaviour the book's going to teach Gary is *'prudence.'* What does this word mean?

   Prudence, is behaviour that thinks with God's wisdom *before* acting.

The opposite of prudence is when we run gun-ho into something without thinking through the consequences. I think we've all probably been there in our lives. We've all probably rushed into a decision at one time or another without thinking through the consequences.

As a new Christian, the Bible says that <u>Gary is going to have to relearn how to live his life</u> and make decisions as a Jesus follower now. **It's going to be hard** and **it won't come naturally** because he's been so used to living life his way and on his own terms.

3X *'...for giving prudence to those who are simple, knowledge and discretion to the young – let the wise listen and add to their learning, and let the discerning get guidance – for understanding proverbs and parables, the sayings and riddles of the wise.'* **Proverbs 1:4-6**

GARY

Gary has never heard of the word 'prudence,' let alone lived prudently. His whole life has been lived according to his emotions at any given time. He flies off the handle when provoked. He runs headlong into making decisions without thinking of the consequences.

In the past, when his son annoyed him he would get mad, and sometimes even react violently...

In the past, when his pals tempted him with anything he'd say yes just to be part of the crowd...

He has debts from maxing out his credit cards. He owes loan sharks and owes money everywhere from bad drug deals to buying cars he can't afford.

STOP

Q: What would it look like for Gary to now begin to live prudently? How could he begin to 'think wisely before acting' in these areas of his life?

 '...for giving prudence to those who are simple, knowledge and discretion to the young — let the wise listen and add to their learning, and let the discerning get guidance — for understanding proverbs and parables, the sayings and riddles of the wise.' **Proverbs 1:4-6**

Notice who the book of Proverbs has been written for.

The simple
The young
The wise

Who does he mean by 'the simple'? Is he talking about people who aren't very bright? No. He's talking about those, like Gary, who are <u>new to the</u>

faith. He's talking to those who are <u>inexperienced</u> when it comes to reading their Bibles and understanding what church is all about.

But he's also talking to *the young* who, Proverbs tells us, need a lot of wisdom because they are often fools. These are the kinds of people who are <u>not very teachable</u>. They think they know all the answers, often before they even understand the questions! They tend to be <u>unwise</u> in their choice of friends and they seem to <u>constantly give in</u> to sexual temptation and lust. They <u>live for the moment</u> and they don't care about eternal things.

Finally, Proverbs is also for the *wise*. Many Christians get comfortable the longer they go on in the Christian life. After a while, once they have a bit of knowledge under their belt, they begin to think they've arrived. They begin to think of the good news about Jesus and discipleship as things for *'baby believers'*. But they fail to realise that:

A Christian is *always* learning, *always* teachable.
A mature Christian is eager to *add* to their learning.
A wise Christian is *always aware* of how easy it is to fall into foolish thinking and behaviour.

GARY

When Gary goes to church he feels like everyone else in the room is 'fine.' He feels like he's the only one in the room struggling with the voices warring in his head. He feels completely out of place.

Gary needs to know that not everybody is fine. In fact, everybody is going through the same experience as he is but just at different levels and with different issues. **Gary needs to understand that everybody struggles to live wisely and prudently**.

 'The fear of the Lord is the beginning of knowledge, but fools despise wisdom and instruction.' **Proverbs 1:7**

ILLUSTRATION

What do we do once we have learned the basics of the alphabet? We begin forming words. Then we begin forming sentences. Then paragraphs. What do we do when we learn the basics of mathematics? We put it into practice by counting and dividing and subtracting. In fact mathematics comes in pretty handy when we are handling money and paying our bills! The point is we learn the basics and then we begin to apply them to our daily lives. Soon we just write and shop and pay bills instinctively because the basics behind them are drilled into our minds.

The point is if we are going to learn how to apply *wisdom* in our daily lives, then we better get the basics right. If we want to get to a stage in our lives when applying wisdom and prudence to all our decisions is second nature, then we have to burn the basics behind it into our souls. So here's the question:

> *If the basics behind writing is learning the alphabet*
> > *If the basics behind handling money is learning mathematics*

<u>What are the basics behind acting wisely and prudently in the Christian life?</u>

Here's the surprise. Here's what you might not expect. The answer to Gary's problem, according to the book of Proverbs, is *fear*. But what is *'the fear of the Lord'*? In the Bible the 'fear of the Lord' is a two-sided coin.

First, there's the fear of God for those who are not in a right relationship to God.

<u>This fear is terror.</u>

It is a frightening terror because our sin makes us liable to the judgment of God. We can go through the first couple of pages of the Bible when Adam and Eve rebel against God, but when they hear God walking in the garden they hide terrified <u>because they know they're going to face God's judgment</u>.

Those who are sinners in rebellion against God *ought to be terrified* of this God. In **Isaiah 33:14** we hear sinners crying in terror *'who of us can dwell with the consuming fire, who of us can dwell with everlasting burning?'*

If you're not a Christian
> you may be afraid of nothing,
>> you may be afraid of everything,
>>> **but you must fear this one thing:**

<u>One terrifying day you will face the consequences of your rebellion against the creator.</u>

3X *'It is a dreadful thing to fall into the hands of the living God.'* **Hebrews 10:31**

GARY

Gary's confused. He's thinking, *'But that's why I became a Christian. That fear of God's judgment was what drove me to trust that when Jesus died on the cross he took that judgment in my place. So surely now I don't have to fear God.'*

STOP

Q: *What do you think? Is Gary right? How would you answer him?*

Gary needs to understand that there is a second fear of the Lord — for those in right relationship to Him.

Gary's right, <u>he no longer has to fear God's judgment for his sin</u>. **But**, the Bible is clear, even <u>now his relationship with the Lord is to be one of 'fear.'</u> That's not just true in the Old Testament in books like Proverbs, but also in the New Testament.

3X *'Since you call on a Father who judges each person's work impartially, live out your time as foreigners here in reverent fear.'* **1 Peter 1:17**

'Show proper respect to everyone, love the family of believers, fear God, honour the emperor.' **1 Peter 2:17**

'Therefore, my dear friends, as you have always obeyed—not only in my presence, but now much more in my absence—continue to work out your salvation with fear and trembling.' **Philippians 2:12**

In other words, <u>God's people</u> are to be <u>God-fearers</u>.

But, Gary's question still stands. **If Jesus saves us from our sins and from the wrath of God to come, why exactly do we need to fear the Lord?**

Well, we may well be saved but that does not mean that we can take our new found peace with God for granted. In the book of Proverbs God is mentioned ninety-four times and in eighty-seven of those times He is given the title, *The Lord*.

When it comes to our relationship with the Lord, we must **never forget** exactly who our relationship is with and what side of the relationship we're on.

He's the Creator. *We're created.*
He's eternal. *We're here today, gone tomorrow.*
He's holy. *We're sinful.*
He's the Saviour. *We're the desperately needy.*
He's the Father. *We're His sons and daughters.*

> **See who He is?**
> > *See who we are?*
> > > <u>See what side of the relationship we're on?</u>

<u>That impacts how we relate to Him</u>.

<u>And that impacts how we think and how we act</u>.

We don't make the rules.
We don't pull the strings.
We don't call the shots.

We bow down and worship Him.
We stand in awe of Him.
We humbly obey Him.
We deeply respect Him.

In short, we 'fear' Him.

Think back to where we started this chapter. If the supply teacher's in the room, we behave in one way; If the headmaster's in the room, we behave another way; If a policeman's in the room, we behave in a certain way; If someone we're attracted to is in the room, we behave a different way; If our gran is in the room, we behave in a different way.

Much of Gary's behaviour is driven by fear. He fears letting his pastor down so he keeps plugging away at church. But he also fears his dad, and so when he's around him he plays down how serious he's taking this Christian stuff. He really fears what his mates think of him, and so he denies how much time he's spending with Christians and lies about where he's been to try to preserve his reputation.

STOP

Q: *How would Gary's behaviour change in all of these areas if he really learned 'the fear of the Lord?'*

Knowing that we are in a relationship with the Lord, and knowing what side of the relationship we are on, means we know that the Lord's in every room.

He's everywhere.
He sees everything.
He hears everything.
He knows everything.

Gary's biggest problem, and ours, is that <u>we fear the wrong person</u>. The biggest factor that controls or changes our behaviour should not be dependent on the relationship we have with whoever walks in the room next, but on our relationship with <u>the Lord who is unchanging and everywhere</u>.

Gary's problems stem from the fact that he's been behaving like a chameleon. He's been acting differently around different people. He's been constantly working out where he is in the pecking order depending on who is in front of him. If he fears them, he falls into line. If he doesn't fear them, he'll make them fear him. He's found himself becoming pretty two-faced. <u>Imagine the difference in his life and his relationships if he began to truly fear the Lord over all other people in his life</u>.

GARY
How do I start? What do I do?

Again, we go back to the beginning, the 'ABC', the '123', and we look once more at the cross of Jesus. It's at the foot of the cross that we realise <u>the full terror of what our sins deserve</u>. It is at the foot of the cross that we stand in total awe of <u>The Lord Almighty who is to be feared above all</u>.

When Gary looks at the cross of Jesus he sees a God who he should love *and* fear.

> He is awesome, and holy, and righteous.
> > But He is also gracious, and forgiving, and merciful.

This is the place where Gary entered into a relationship with Him; but there is no doubt which side of the relationship Gary is on.

✗ **MEMORY VERSE**
'The fear of the Lord is the beginning of knowledge, but fools despise wisdom and instruction.' **Proverbs 1:7**

SUMMARY

Gary, listen, my son. You need to make wise and prudent choices in every area of life. The only way you're going to do this is to get wisdom from the only Wise King – God – and learn how to fear Him.

WHAT'S THE POINT?

LISTENING TO THE WRONG VOICE WILL LEAVE ME TRAPPED, BUT GOD'S VOICE WILL SHOW ME WHERE THE TRAPS ARE.

TWO:
WHO SHOULD I LISTEN TO?

ILLUSTRATION

What was your favourite prank to play on an unsuspecting victim when you were a kid?

> *Bucket of water balanced over a semi-open door...?*
> *Cling-film spread over a toilet seat...?*
> *Maybe the classic two-man prank where one of you crouches down behind someone, and the other person pushes them backwards over you...?*

But, what's the most important factor when setting up a prank?
Secrecy.

If they see the prank being set, they will never fall for it.

3X *'How useless to spread a net where every bird can see it.'* **Proverbs 1:17**

I bet you never thought you were going to get a lesson in bird-catching when you picked up this book. But it's the same principle at play with birds as there is with a prank. If a bird sees the net, the bird avoids the net. But if the hunter hides the net, he's got a decent chance of catching some birds.

In our previous book (WAR) we discussed, in some depth, the traps laid by the **world, the flesh, and the devil**. There's often a danger with our addictions.

> <u>They promise pleasure</u>, but **they hide a deadly net**.
> <u>They promise comfort</u>, but **they disguise slavery**.

They promise life, but **they fast-track death**.

The wages of sin always have been, always will be, death.

But here's what Solomon wants to do in the book of Proverbs: tell us where the hidden traps are. Why does he do this? Because he knows if the bird sees the net, it will avoid the net. And so he makes it his job to point out where all the traps are, so that we can avoid them.

He wants to expose the nets to save us from stumbling.
He wants to bring the trap into full view so we can run away.
He wants to take what could have been fatal and make it useless.

We already know that the Christian life is a dangerous one where we have many enemies. But, the good news is that as
we walk this path
with our Bible in our hands,
we have the voice of King Jesus
to point out where all the deadly traps are.

3⊠ *'My son, if sinful men entice you, do not give in to them. If they say, "**Come along with us**; let's lie in wait for innocent blood, let's ambush some harmless soul; let's swallow them alive, like the grave, and whole, like those who go down to the pit; we will **get all sorts of valuable things** and **fill our houses with plunder**; cast lots with us; **we will all share the loot**" — my son, **do not go along with them, do not set foot on their paths**; for their feet rush into evil, they are swift to shed blood. How useless to spread a net where every bird can see it! These men lie in wait for their own blood; they ambush only themselves! Such are the paths of all who go after ill-gotten gain; **it takes away the life of those who get it**.' **Proverbs 1:10-19**

Here Solomon tells his son a story to show him where one of the most powerful, dangerous traps will be. And it's a little story that should give us a big shock. Why? Because Solomon is warning his own son that, if he's not careful, he could turn into a murderer of innocents. Remember, this is the son of a King. Not just any King. The wisest, richest King on the planet. It doesn't matter whether you're a prince or a pauper, we all have to be on the watch for things in life which can snare us into wicked sin.

This story reveals a powerful, dangerous trap. What's the bait in this trap? What's the temptation for the son to entice him into this net?

It's the thrill of a chase.
It's easy money.
And it's the kick you get out of being one of the lads.

You see? The bait is so tempting. This is everything we love:

a bit of excitement,
    money in your pocket,
        feeling part of the gang.

These other voices will be in our heads.
    These other voices will be loud.
        These other voices will be extremely attractive.
        These other voices will be promising much.

But Solomon knows, it may look very tempting, but it is <u>a deadly trap</u>. He doesn't only show us what it promises to give, but also what it will take away. He tells his son that it will take away his life, in **v. 19**. Solomon exposes the net that would take the son's life. And so he pleads with his son:

Listen, my son,
don't go along with them;
don't set foot on their paths.

GARY

Gary knows something of the thrill of the chase in his own life. The thrill of making easy money in the drugs game. The thrill of being one of the lads fighting at the football games. The thrill of meeting a stranger in a club and getting her into his bed. Before he was a Christian these three things would have been the perfect recipe for a good night out. Gary regularly still gets texts from his old pals - just like the story from Proverbs - asking, 'Come along with us...'

STOP

Q: How does this story help Gary know what to do with these texts?

3X 'Out in the open wisdom calls aloud, she raises her voice in the public square; on top of the wall she cries out, at the city gate she makes her speech: "How long will you who are simple love your simple ways? How long will mockers delight in mockery and fools hate knowledge? Repent at my rebuke! Then I will pour out my thoughts to you, I will make known to you my teachings. But since you refuse to listen when I call and no one pays attention when I stretch out my hand, since you disregard all my advice and do not accept my rebuke, I in turn will laugh when disaster strikes you; I will mock when calamity overtakes you... like a storm, when disaster sweeps over you like a whirlwind, when distress and trouble overwhelm you. Then they will call to me but I will not answer; they will look for me but will not find me, since they hated knowledge and did not choose to fear the Lord. Since they would not accept my advice and spurned my rebuke, they will eat the fruit of their ways and be filled with the fruit of their schemes. For the waywardness of the simple will kill them, and the complacency of fools will destroy them; but whoever listens to me will live in safety and be at ease, without fear of harm."' **Proverbs 1:20-33**

So we've heard Solomon's voice.

And we've heard the voice of those who tempt us towards a trap.

Now, in order to ensure that the voice of God's wisdom is louder in our heads than any other voice, Solomon introduces a woman called Wisdom. We've already seen that God's wisdom will ultimately and perfectly be seen in King Jesus. But, before He arrives on earth, Solomon pictures God's wisdom here as a woman. And the first thing you notice about her is she is loud.

<u>Very loud</u>.

Which, let's face it, <u>is what we need</u>. Her voice joins forces with Solomon's voice to make us face up to the fact that <u>it is vital that we listen to the voices of God's wisdom</u> and avoid the traps that would make us fall back into sin. And she speaks in a way that may come across as brutal and harsh, but she does so deliberately to shock us out of our sinful stupidity. She wants us to know **two things**:

<u>Firstly</u>, if we get caught in these traps the Father is showing us, we need to realise **how hard it is to escape**. Solomon's story was all about an invitation to sin. *Woman Wisdom* now speaks to those who love their sin. She speaks to <u>simple people</u> who love their simple ways. She speaks to <u>mockers</u> who delight in their mockery. The invitation to sin has led to a love of sin. What the father said *'Don't do!'* they now delight in.

We don't just **do** sin.

We **love** sin.

And that's the perverse thing about it: <u>we love the thing that kills us</u>. And when we love it, it's very hard to escape its grip. We've got to see how the story unfolds here:

> *The thing we experiment with today is the thing we're addicted to tomorrow.*
> *And the more we love sin, the less we will love God.*
> *The more we listen to the voice of sin, the more we'll reject the voice of God.*

That's why Solomon was so keen to say *'Listen, my son, don't go along with them!'*

The bottom line is **that if we flirt with sin we'll end up loving it**.

GARY

Gary has often been told by his pastor that becoming a Christian is not just about a new list of do's and don'ts, but it's about changing who and what his heart loves. He's never quite understood that until now. But it's still a battle.

STOP

Q: How will a growing love for God help Gary fight against the temptation to love his old sin?

Secondly, Woman Wisdom wants to show us that **there will be a time when it is too late**. This is where Woman Wisdom gets edgy. She imagines looking at us caught in the trap of sin. She sees us in the disaster and calamity and distress of the trap. And how does she respond?

She laughs at us.
   She mocks us.
      And she does not respond to our cries for help.

That sounds harsh. But God will <u>use all sorts of devices to wake us up</u> if we're being unresponsive to His voice or are unaware of the danger that we're putting ourselves in. Woman Wisdom shouts hard-edged warnings at us now to make us respond so that she won't have to laugh or mock us in the future. We need to hear this.

There will come a time when **it's too late**.
There will come a time when **prayer will be powerless**.

Therefore:
   Respond now.
      Repent now.
         Listen today.
            We don't know if we'll be able to tomorrow.

Sometimes even as Christians we can look at our own sin and think we'll never change. If we're reading this, then there is hope. But we need to **listen**, we need to **wake up**, we need to **act today**.

GARY

Gary often hears the voice in his head that says, 'Just once.' 'Just one more time.' 'This will be the last time.' 'I'll start taking my Christianity seriously tomorrow.'

STOP

Q: What advice would you give to Gary on the basis of what Woman Wisdom has just said? **Proverbs 1:20-33**

Solomon, who's writing these words, knew this stuff first hand. Remember who he was? He was the son of David. Solomon's dad, David, knew how easy it was to fall into a trap of sin, knew how quickly even a wise, rich king could become a murderer. We can read the story in **2 Samuel 11**. King David saw a beautiful woman bathing.

That led to lust in his heart.
    That led to sleeping with the woman in his bed.
        That led to the conception of Solomon.
            That led to telling lies to her husband.
                That led to him setting a trap for the husband on a
                    battlefield.
                That led to the husband lying dead in a tomb.

The tragedy is that Solomon fell into exactly the same trap (we can read about that in **1 Kings 11**). The truth is, we all do. The story Solomon tells in Proverbs 1 is a trap that we've all fallen into.

    That's why we need a king greater than David.
        That's why we need a king greater than Solomon.

Jesus is the only one who plays a different actor in the story.

Where we all play the son who jumps in with the plot to make some easy money, Jesus plays the role of the man who is attacked and killed.

> **His is the innocent blood spilt.**
> **His is the harmless soul ambushed.**
> **He is the one swallowed alive by the grave.**

But He does so in order that He might take the disaster and calamity and distress that our foolish sin deserves.

> *The strike of disaster hits him,*
> > *he is overtaken by calamity,*
> > > *he is overwhelmed by trouble and distress,*

all so that we – if we repent of our sin, and listen to His voice – can live in safety, at ease, without fear of harm.

 MEMORY VERSE

'For the waywardness of the simple will kill them, and the complacency of fools will destroy them; but whoever listens to me will live in safety and be at ease, without fear of harm.' **Proverbs 1:32-33**

 SUMMARY

Gary, listen, my son. The Christian life is dangerous, and you've got many enemies. But with the Bible in your hands you'll have the voice of King Jesus to point out where the deadly traps are. But beware: if you're caught, it's hard to escape; and there will come a time when it's too late.

WHAT'S THE POINT?

IN A DANGEROUS WORLD, GOD WILL PROTECT YOU BY PUTTING HIS WISDOM DEEP IN YOUR HEART.

THREE:
WHO'S GOT MY BACK?

GARY

Growing up Gary knew that to stay safe he had to know the right people. He knew how to handle himself, but learned from an early age that it was always worth knowing the right lads who would have your back. However, Gary's beginning to understand that being a Christian means that not all fights are physical. He realises that he is going to need some spiritual backup in this life too. But at the moment he's not too sure what that is going to look like. He can build a reputation to care for his house and family on the scheme. And he can go to the boxing gym to make sure he can take care of himself. But now he's asking you, 'What do I need to do to guard myself spiritually?'

ILLUSTRATION

I once knew a man who had two sons. His two sons had the same childhood – same dad; same rules; same advice. One son recently graduated from university with a law degree. The other son is an alcoholic with a criminal record, living in a locked ward of a hospital. What happened? Both sons **heard** exactly the same things. But only one son actually **listened**.

There's a massive difference between hearing someone's words and accepting someone's words. Likewise, there is a huge difference between <u>hearing</u> wisdom and <u>being</u> wise. There's a world of difference between wisdom in our ears and wisdom in our hearts.

'My son, if you accept my words and store up my commands within you, turning your ear to wisdom and applying your heart to understanding – indeed, **if** you call out for insight and cry aloud for understanding, and if

you look for it as for silver and search for it as for hidden treasure, **then** *you will understand the fear of the Lord and find the knowledge of God.'*
Proverbs 2:1-5

We've seen already in **Proverbs 1:7** that *'the fear of the LORD is the beginning of knowledge'.* In these verses he's telling us how we get there: *'if you... if you... if you...* **then** *you will understand the fear of the Lord and find the knowledge of God.'*

So what exactly does it look like to *get wisdom?*

> We don't just *listen* to it. We've got to *accept* it **(v. 1)**.
> That's the difference between *receiving an instruction book* and actually *doing what it tells you to do.* We don't just *accept* it, but we've got to *store* it up **(v. 1)**.
> That's the difference between *forgetting* it and *memorising* it.
>
> We don't just *store it up,* but you've got to *turn your ear* to it **(v. 2)**.
> That's the difference between hearing it as *one voice* among *many* and hearing it as *the most important voice* in our life.
>
> We don't just *turn our ear* to it, but we *apply our heart* **(v. 2)**.
> That's the difference between *listening* to a voice and actually *loving* someone's voice.

We've got to get the wisdom of God into our heart.

But how do we do that? Well, twice we're told to *'cry aloud'* for it. So far it's been Woman Wisdom who's been crying aloud in Proverbs. Now it's our turn to get vocal.

> **This is something you need to pray and ask God for.**
> > *It's not something that's natural to us.*
> > *It's something that's outside of us.*
> **To get it in our heart we're going to have to get on our knees.**

Twice we're told 'look for it as for silver' and 'search for it as for hidden treasure.' In other words, God's wisdom is priceless. At the Queen's coronation in 1953 she was handed a Bible and told, 'We present you with this book, the most valuable thing that this world affords.' What If I told you I'd hidden a billion pounds in your neighbourhood? What would you do? I'm assuming you wouldn't rest till you found it, right? Well, to get God's wisdom we need to search for it as if it were worth more than anything else. To get this it needs to be our everything; we've got to be <u>all-in</u>.

The problem is that we live in a culture where we applaud the lazy. We congratulate those who can get as much as possible with as little effort as possible. But, that does not translate to the Christian life. Wisdom will not be achieved by laziness. We will only get it *in our heart* when we pursue it with *all of our heart* (**Jer. 29:13**).

STOP

Q: In his past, Gary definitely would have fitted into that laziness culture. What do you think **Proverbs 2:1-5** would look like in Gary's life on a day-to-day basis?

3X 'For the Lord gives wisdom; from his mouth come knowledge and understanding.' **Proverbs 2:6**

Now, even though wisdom is something we're to *get*, it is also something that we're *given*. Any knowledge of God, or wisdom for living, is a gift given by God.

It's not earned.
It's not achieved.
It's not something to brag about.

We can only accept His words because He has given us His words.
We can only store up His commands because He has given us His commands.
We can only turn our ear to wisdom because He has given us His wisdom.

That's why we need to pray for it. Because we realise it must come from outside of ourselves. Why does God give us His wisdom when we ask for it?

 *'He holds success in store for the upright, he is a **shield** to those whose walk is blameless, for he **guards** the course of the just and **protects** the way of his faithful ones. Then you will understand what is right and just and fair – every good path. For **wisdom will enter your heart**, and knowledge will be pleasant to your soul. Discretion will **protect** you, and understanding will **guard** you. **Wisdom will save** you from the ways of wicked men, from men whose words are perverse, who have left the straight paths to walk in dark ways, who delight in doing wrong and rejoice in the perverseness of evil, whose paths are crooked and who are devious in their ways. **Wisdom will save you** also from the adulterous woman, from the wayward woman with her seductive words, who has left the partner of her youth and ignored the covenant she made before God. Surely her house leads down to death and her paths to the spirits of the dead. None who go to her return or attain the paths of life. Thus you will walk in the ways of the good and keep to the paths of the righteous. For the upright will live in the land, and the blameless will remain in it; but the wicked will be cut off from the land, and the unfaithful will be torn from it.'* **Proverbs 2:7-22**

 ## ILLUSTRATION

If your school playground was anything like mine, you'll have probably been involved in the kind of argument that went something like: *'My dad's bigger than your dad.' 'Aye, well my dad could beat up your dad.'* And so on, and so forth, for the rest of break-time. *All this reveals is that even as children we have an instinct in us to call for backup when life gets rough.*

<u>Protection is necessary when danger is a reality</u>. And in Proverbs 2, Solomon is certain about the clear and present dangers facing the son:

> Wicked men who will lead him on a path of darkness (**vv. 12-15**).
> A whore who will tempt him into sexual oblivion (**vv. 16-19**).

Solomon is just as certain, however, that although the danger is real, God will shield, guard, and protect the lives of His people.

He's on our side.
He's got our back.
Our heavenly dad can and will beat their dad.
He will guard us.

What may be surprising is the way he will guard us. If it were up to us, God's protection of us would probably involve some kind of lightning bolts from heaven zapping our enemies, or ninja-angels kicking Satan's head in when he comes to tempt us, or some amazing celebrity-preacher come to give us a motivational speech when we're about to give in to sin. God's plan is different. And better. Surprising even...

 'For wisdom will enter your heart, and knowledge will be pleasant to your soul. Discretion will protect you, and understanding will guard you.' **Proverbs 2:10-11**

It is not just that God's wisdom guards us. It is God's wisdom *in us* that guards us. It is not something external to us, but internal. In other words, the Lord often protects us from the inside-out.

 ILLUSTRATION

The parents of a teenage boy find out that he has smashed his brand new iPhone. The parents saved for ages and shelled out a lot of cash for that phone. Both are faced with the same temptation. The dad flies off the handle in an angry rage, grabs the boy by the scruff of the neck and screams at him. The mum calmly and patiently asks the son how it happened. On finding out it was a mistake she forgives him. Same situation. Same temptation. Different responses? Why? It's a matter of the heart.

The heart is the issue.

Our character
Our discretion (that is, our ability to make good choices)
Our foolishness

The issue is we are fools that despise wisdom and instruction.

The message of the Bible is *not* that we simply have to try and change our behaviour. That we must try to keep to the rules. Simply imposing Christian behaviour on someone with a heart like this is like feeding nuts to a person with a nut allergy. It's only going to make them ill. The message of the Bible is that God not only forgives and removes our guilt and shame and sin by Jesus' death. It is not only that He credits us with a perfect record of law-keeping through Jesus' life. But, it is that <u>He gives us a new heart</u>.

A heart that not only loves to listen to His voice,
    but a heart that is able to obey His voice.

3X *'I will give them a heart to know me, that I am the Lord. They will be my people, and I will be their God, for they will return to me with all their heart.'*
Jeremiah 24:7

So God protects us, guards us, from the inside-out. He puts His wisdom *within us*, so that having a **knowledge** of Him is more pleasant to us than our sin; **discretion** protects us from making stupid choices; **understanding** guards us from walking the path that leads to death.

God's voice does not just remain outside of us. It is not like a voice we hear audibly with our ears. It enters into our hearts so that it becomes something that speaks to us deep inside.

That's why growing as a Christian, maturing as a Christian is so important. It's the way God guards us. <u>God guards us by making us more like Jesus</u>. So that, whereas when I first became a Christian and I bumped into the guys in **verses 12-15** who delight in the deviousness of their dark ways, I probably would have gone along with them. Now though, as God has given me more knowledge and discretion and understanding, I know not to hang around with them.

<u>His wisdom in me *saves* me</u>.

So that whereas when I first became a Christian and I bumped into the woman in **vv. 16-19** offering me seductive words and an invite to her bedroom, I probably would have jumped right in. Now though, as God has given me more knowledge and discretion and understanding, I know that her house leads down to death.

His wisdom in me saves me.

GARY

A few months ago – not long after he became a Christian – if Gary had bumped into one of his pals on the high street, he knows that it more than likely would have led to an invitation back into his old lifestyle. And he probably would have accepted the invite. But, when it happened today – same pal, same high street – he saw it as an opportunity to share the impact that Jesus had had on his life. What has changed?

What has changed is that Gary is being saved from the inside-out. The Spirit of God is transforming him as he prays to God for wisdom to make the right choices and to guard him against temptation and sin. Also, he knows that God has got his back in any and every situation. That gives him the confidence to live for Jesus and be a good witness to the world around him.

 MEMORY VERSE
'For wisdom will enter your heart, and knowledge will be pleasant to your soul. Discretion will protect you, and understanding will guard you.'
Proverbs 2:10-11

 SUMMARY
Gary, listen, my son. Protection's necessary when danger is a reality. Although the danger is real, God will shield, guard, and protect you. And He protects you from the inside-out as He puts His wisdom into your heart and makes you more like Jesus.

WHAT'S THE POINT?

THE HEART OF SIN IS TRUSTING IN MYSELF, AND SO THE HEART OF BECOMING AND LIVING AS A CHRISTIAN IS TURNING FROM THAT AND TRUSTING IN GOD.

FOUR:
WHO CAN I TRUST?

RECAP

Every Christian needs God's wisdom to live for Jesus in this world.
The path we walk in life is full of hidden traps.
God has got our backs and will protect us if we listen and obey His voice.

GARY

Gary's life has completely changed. He'd still recognise himself in the mirror from a year ago. But in terms of his life, his character, his temper, his language, his relationships, he's unrecognisable. He is trying to follow God's ways in everything he does. But every day, in every decision, there are still loads of voices tempting him to return to the old way of doing things. He knows that leaning on his own understanding had left his life in a complete mess. No doubt about that. But it was easier back then. And that's the pull...

From **Proverbs 3** we're now going to look at three areas where Gary feels the pull back to the old school Gary most intensely:

How he uses his money.
How he responds to discipline.
How he treats people around him.

If we were to read through Proverbs 3 we would not miss the fact that if we live *wisely* then we'll also live *well*. <u>Wisdom never comes to the party alone</u>. She always brings her pals. And who she brings in Proverbs 3 are:

Life
    Prosperity
        Favour
            Blessing
                Riches
                      Honour
                Peace
            Safety
        Sleep
    Confidence
Grace

That's cool, right? *But*, what if we've not been wise? What if we have been a bit foolish?

Proverbs 3 also says that our foolishness brings its own pals to the party. They are:

death
    poverty
        curse
    war
  fear
shame

This is the problem we've seen all along in Proverbs.

Wisdom brings *life*.

But, our foolishness brings *death*.

 'She is a **tree of life** *to those who take hold of her; those who hold her fast will be blessed.'* **Proverbs 3:18**

This is Solomon talking about Woman Wisdom again, and he describes her as *'a tree of life.'*

That tree has come up in the Bible before. That tree was in the <u>Garden of Eden</u> where Adam and Eve lived (**Gen. 2:9**). That tree was the <u>source of life for Adam and Eve</u> and they could eat from it whenever they wanted. But, when they rebelled against God, they were <u>thrown out</u> of Eden. They were <u>barred</u> from access to the tree of life. They were <u>banned</u>.

They had <u>restraining orders</u> on them not allowing them anywhere near it. In fact, God placed bodyguard angels and a flashing sword to guard the way to the tree of life (**Gen. 3:24**).

It's the Proverbs 3 problem again.

Obedience brings *life* – access to the tree of life *granted*.

But, our disobedience brings *death* – access to the tree of life *denied*.

We've seen that God has a solution to solve our problem: <u>God sent His son Jesus to die on a tree of death to give us access again to the tree of life</u>. Which is why that tree not only comes up at the start of the Bible in **Genesis 2:9**, but it comes up again at the end of the Bible in **Revelation 22:2**. In God's New Creation - for those who trust in Jesus:

The bans will be lifted
The restraining orders removed
The bodyguards will be unemployed
We will have access to the tree of life once more. **Forever**.

But what do we do until then? Well, Solomon says, in Eden the way to life was to eat from the tree of life; in the New Creation the way to life will be to eat from the tree of life; but in the meantime, the way to life is to <u>listen to the words of Woman Wisdom</u>.

We'd be wrong if we thought we'd have to wait until the New Creation to get our teeth stuck into some of that juicy fruit. We can get stuck in today simply by opening our Bible.

'Trust in the Lord with all your heart and lean not on your own understanding; in all your ways submit to him, and he will make your paths straight.'
Proverbs 3:5-6

Christians love these verses. They quote them all the time. What we often don't realise is that these words get right to the heart of our sinfulness. The heart of sin is that we:

> **don't** trust God,
>> we follow our **own** understanding,
>>> we **don't** submit to God,
>>>> and so we tread our **own** path towards death.

We're like the men who are too proud to ask anyone for directions when they're lost in the car. We'll drive round and round in circles instead of asking somebody for help. Why? Because we don't want to look weak or stupid. Even when we do ask people for *'advice'* we're still trusting ourselves. Often we're not even truly seeking advice. We're simply looking for someone to tell us to do exactly what we've already decided we're going to do. And we'll keep asking different people until we get the answer that we've already decided we want. We're sneaky, right?

The world's voices tell us *'believe in yourself,' 'if it feels right it can't be wrong,' 'follow your heart.'* And so <u>we trust</u> **ourselves, our opinions, our experience, our wisdom**. We do things **our way**.

The voice in Proverbs, however, tells us, 'Listen, my son, *you're a fool. Don't trust yourself. Trust God.'* That is why these verses not only get to the heart of our sin, they also get to the heart of what it means to be a Christian.

<u>Negatively</u>, it means confessing and repenting of our lack of trust in God, and saying to God that we're not going to lean on our own understanding anymore. <u>Positively</u>, it means trusting God and the gospel with all of our heart, and submitting to God in all of our ways. <u>It's all or nothing</u>. We're either all-in or all-out. <u>We can't lean in two directions at one time.</u>

Someone once said to me that if they became a Christian they didn't think that much in their life would change. That told me that they didn't understand anything about their sin or anything about what it meant to be a Christian. When we stop leaning on our own understanding, and we start trusting God, it means that the deciding factor in **every single decision**, of every single day of your life, is now someone other than us.

We now trust God with all of our heart.
We now lean on God's understanding.
We now submit all our ways to God's ways.
We now walk the path that God wants us to walk.

Everything's changed!

3X *'Honour the Lord with your wealth, with the firstfruits of all your crops; then your barns will be filled to overflowing, and your vats will brim over with new wine.'* **Proverbs 3:9-10**

Here's the first question Proverbs 3 asks us: **How do we use our money?**

Christians love a bit of **Proverbs 3:5-6** around the house! They stick it on cards. They hang it up in their hallways. They buy fridge magnets. One thing I have never seen on a fridge magnet is **Proverbs 3:9-10**. Why not? Well, we love the idea of a straight path through life. But, we're less keen on the idea of giving our money away. Yet, Solomon says we are to 'honour' God with our wealth. 'Honour' has the idea of weightiness or heaviness. That means, that the heaviest, the biggest factor in how a Christian gets or uses their money, is whether it pleases or displeases God.

Probably, before we were Christians, the heaviest influence on *how we got* our money was something like:

Well everyone else is screwing the social security system, so I'm entitled to as well.
Or, as long as I'm not hurting anyone I'm happy to bend the rules a bit to get by.

Nothing wrong with a little cash in hand. The tax man will never miss it.

Probably, before we were Christians, the heaviest influence on *how we spent* our money was something like:

I need to be seen by others as wearing the right clothes, having the newest stuff.

Or, it's blowing cash chasing experiences on nights out that I can't remember.

Proverbs say that the heaviest influence on both how we get money and how we spend our money should be God. That's why it talks about *'firstfruits.'* That means our first and our best, not just giving God our leftovers and our sloppy seconds. We shouldn't treat God like a vulture who just gets to pick at the bones of a carcass once the lions have had their share. He gets first dibs. It's like the girl I know who, when she became a Christian, the first thing she did when she got her next pay cheque was give 10 per cent to her church. She didn't buy what she wanted and then see what was left to give away. God came first. Everything else in her life got the leftovers.

And we can't use the excuse that says, *'It says honour God with your wealth, but I'm not wealthy, so this doesn't apply to me.'* In **Mark 12:41-44** we read, *'Jesus sat down opposite the place where the offerings were put and watched the crowd putting their money into the temple treasury. Many rich people threw in large amounts. But a poor widow came and put in two very small copper coins, worth only a few pence. Calling his disciples to him, Jesus said, 'Truly I tell you, this poor widow has put **more** into the treasury than all the others. They all gave out of their wealth; but she, out of her poverty, **put in everything** – **all** she had to live on.'*

What matters is not the *act.*
Nor the *amount.*
But, the *attitude* of the heart.

GARY

Gary and his partner are absolute experts in playing the social security system. They know what the different kinds of benefits are and exactly how much they are 'entitled' to. Although they live together, as far as the government is concerned they each live in different houses. Why? So that they can claim more money from the housing department! Gary will do absolutely anything to earn some quick cash. He's been known to play the loan-shark – charging high interest and sending the heavies round if people don't pay. And if some stuff that 'fell off the back of a lorry' happened to end up in his hands, he wouldn't miss the opportunity to make a few quid here and there.

STOP

Q: What's it going to look like for Gary to 'honour God with his wealth' now that he's become a Christian?

Here's the second question Proverbs 3 asks us: **how do we respond to discipline?**

 'My son, do not despise the Lord's discipline, and do not resent his rebuke, because the Lord disciplines those he loves, as a father the son he delights in.' **Proverbs 3:11-12**

In these verses Solomon introduces us to two massively important truths:

> God disciplines His children.
> God disciplines His children because He **loves** His children.

For some of us the idea of God disciplining us as His children is very hard to get our heads around because we have had such a bad experience of our earthly parents abusing us. But, the Bible's view of God's discipline is not of God flying off the handle in uncontrolled anger simply to hurt or get back at His children. Instead, the Bible's view of God's discipline is of a careful, controlled, purposeful training of character, **always done out of a heart of love**.

God's discipline is not like an episode of Itchy and Scratchy on the Simpsons, where God is like the sadistic mouse dreaming up hysterical ways to destroy the helpless cat. God's discipline is more like that of Mr Miyagi in the Karate Kid, who carefully and patiently trains Daniel. Although he doesn't understand it at the time, Daniel comes to realise that all Mr Miyagi's enforced fence-painting and car-washing have equipped him to defend himself against his attackers.

> *Like gold refined in a fire.*
> *Or diamonds created under pressure.*
> *Or muscles grown through resistance.*
> *Or plants flowering after pruning.*

Christians are made wise through the Lord's loving discipline.

 'Endure hardship as discipline; God is treating you as his children... No discipline seems pleasant at the time, but painful. Later on, however, it produces a harvest of righteousness and peace for those who have been trained by it.' **Hebrews 12:7, 11**

God disciplines us <u>because He loves us</u>. Asking for Him *not* to discipline us is actually asking for *less* of God's love, not *more*. The hardships of life are the times when we are tempted to despise God: stop trusting Him, start leaning on our own understanding, and try and walk our own path to avoid the hardships. Solomon warns us: Listen, my son, don't despise His discipline. It is a sign that He loves you. It is the means by which He is making you wise.

GARY

The behaviour of Gary's teenage son is out of control. He's constantly getting into trouble at school. He's defiant at home – disobeying Gary and saying horrible stuff to his mum. It's doing Gary's nut in, causing major stress, and it's now making Gary and his partner fight all the time. Before Gary was a Christian he would have reacted in the same way his dad did when he stepped out of line as a kid – give him a right good kicking.

STOP

Q: How should these verses about the Lord's discipline affect how Gary disciplines his son? How should Gary respond to this hardship in his life, knowing that the Lord disciplines those He loves, and from what we read in Hebrews 12?

3X 'Do not withhold good from those to whom it is due, when it is in your power to act. Do not say to your neighbour, "Come back tomorrow and I'll give it to you" – when you already have it with you. Do not plot harm against your neighbour, who lives trustfully near you. Do not accuse anyone for no reason – when they have done you no harm. Do not envy the violent or choose any of their ways.' **Proverbs 3:27-31**

Here's the third question Woman Wisdom asks us: **how do we treat our neighbours?**

How we treat our neighbours, according to the Bible, will reveal a huge amount about how much we love God. Jesus says, in **Mark 12:29-31**: 'The most important [commandment],' answered Jesus, 'is this: "Hear, O Israel: The Lord our God, the Lord is one. Love the Lord your God with all your heart and with all your soul and with all your mind and with all your strength." The second is this: "Love your neighbour as yourself." There is no commandment greater than these.' Jesus also explains in **Luke 10:25-37** that our 'neighbours' are not just those who stay immediately next door to us, but anyone who crosses our path who's in need.

There is a famous Australian soap-opera called Neighbours. The theme tune goes something like this.

'Neighbours, everybody needs good neighbours
With a little understanding, you can find the perfect blend
Neighbours, should be there for one another
That's when good neighbours become good friends.'

That's all well and good when our neighbours are good, understanding, and there for one another. Walking wisely would be easy if all the people who crossed our path were like that! But what happens when our neighbours are a nightmare, irrational, and provocative? That would make for a very different theme tune!

We need the *'do not'* commands in **Proverbs 3:27-31** precisely because we are prone to do these very things:

> *Lie to our neighbours to preserve our own comfort.*
> *Plot against our neighbours to get our revenge.*
> *Envy our neighbours and their way of life.*

Solomon knows that those closest to us will be the hardest to live with. But he also knows that we can't claim to love God whilst hating our brother or sister or neighbour (**1 John 2:9-11**). Here's what we need to learn:

Wisdom will be proved in community;
> *Wisdom will be exercised when we are asked to love the unlovable;*
>> *Wisdom will be tested when we are provoked by the sins of others;*
>>> *Wisdom will be judged when we are confronted by someone's need.*
>>>> *Our love for God will be demonstrated in our love for our neighbours – whoever they might be, and whatever they do.*

Gary never would have thought that <u>the key to a fulfilled life</u> would be found **not in trusting in himself**, **giving** his money away, inviting **discipline**, and **loving the unlovely**. However, he also never thought that all the promises and pleasures of his former life would have left his life in such a mess. That's why he, and we, <u>need to listen to God's voice in order to hear God's wisdom</u>. It's not always what we would expect. But it's **always** the way to life.

For example:

*Who would have thought God would display His wisdom in the
foolishness of a cross?*
*Who would have thought God would display His strength in the
weakness of a cross?*

3X *'The message of the cross is foolishness to those who are perishing, but
to us who are being saved it is the power of God... Christ the power of
God and the wisdom of God. For the foolishness of God is wiser than
human wisdom, and the weakness of God is stronger than human strength.'*
1 Corinthians 1:18, 24-25

God knows what He's doing. His thoughts are not our thoughts.
His ways are not our ways. So we *must always* listen to His voice.

⚒ MEMORY VERSE

*'She is a tree of life to those who take hold of her; those who hold her fast
will be blessed.'* **Proverbs 3:18**

⦿ SUMMARY

*Gary, listen, my son. If you try and do things your way and on your
own you'll get nowhere. You've got to trust God with all that you are, in
everything that you do. And that will be seen very clearly in how you use
your money, how you respond to discipline, and how you relate to those
closest to you.*

WHAT'S THE POINT?

EVERYTHING YOU DO FLOWS FROM YOUR HEART, SO GUARD IT ABOVE ALL ELSE.

FIVE:
WHAT'S MOST IMPORTANT?

 'Above all else, guard your heart, for everything you do flows from it.'
Proverbs 4:23

 ILLUSTRATION

A few years ago my father-in-law had a heart attack that resulted in him needing a quadruple heart-bypass. Until something like that happens you don't think much about your heart. We kind of take it for granted. We're the selfie generation who are madly obsessed with the outward appearance for the sake of a decent post on Instagram, but we think very little about our heart. Which is stupid, because everything we do flows from the life-blood that our hearts pump round our body.

From the Bible's point of view, the *'heart'* is not just the physical, pink-coloured, beating thing in the middle of your chest. When the Bible speaks of our *'heart'* it's speaking of our innermost being, our core personality, the source of our behaviour, thoughts, and emotions. <u>The heart is at the core of who we are as people</u>.

As **Proverbs 4:23** says, *'everything you do flows from it.'* Our heart – what it loves, what it demands, what it craves, what it hates – is engaged in everything we do. We know this. For example, why, when we buy a new outfit, do we feel different when we wear it out for the first time? All clothing does is cover what needs to be covered for the sake of public decency (most of the time!). <u>Yet we take clothing and we make it the source of our dignity</u>. Why, when we get a new hair-cut, do we walk out of the barbers with a bigger swagger than when we walked in? After all a haircut is only maintenance – like cutting the grass in our garden. <u>But we take it and make it the source of our confidence</u>.

What's going on?

Our heart is engaged in *everything* we do — from our clothing to our hairstyle to our *everything*. That is why Solomon writes, *'Above all else, guard your heart.'* Not only does everything we do flow from it, but:

> Our heart is what God **desires** — *'love the Lord your God with all your heart...'* (**Matt. 22:37**).
> Our heart is what God **sees** — *'People look at the outward appearance, but the Lord looks at the heart'* (**1 Sam. 16:7**).
> Our heart is what God **will judge** — *'He will bring to light what is hidden in darkness and will expose the motives of the heart'* (**1 Cor. 4:5**).

So, we need to guard it like airport security — checking everything that **comes in**; and checking everything that **comes out**. Let's look at how **Proverbs 4** helps Gary guard his heart.

 'Listen, my sons, to a father's instruction; pay attention and gain understanding. I give you sound learning, so do not forsake my teaching. For I too was a son to my father, still tender, and cherished by my mother. Then he taught me, and he said to me, "Take hold of my words with all your heart; keep my commands, and you will live. Get wisdom, get understanding; do not forget my words or turn away from them. Do not forsake wisdom, and she will protect you; love her, and she will watch over you. The beginning of wisdom is this: get wisdom. Though it cost all you have, get understanding. Cherish her, and she will exalt you; embrace her, and she will honour you. She will give you a garland to grace your head and present you with a glorious crown."' **Proverbs 4:1-9**

First, let's think about **GETTING WISDOM INTO OUR HEART**.

This stuff about guarding our heart by getting wisdom sounds a lot like what we looked at in chapter 3. But get used to hearing things over and over again in Proverbs. Solomon knows that

The key to education is repeating yourself.
The key to education is repeating yourself.
The key to education is repeating yourself.

These verses can come across like a man who's thrown a bunch of commands in a semi-automatic rifle and then aimed the barrel at us:

Pay attention! Gain! Don't forsake! Take hold! Keep! Get! Get! Don't forget! Don't forsake! Love! Get! Cherish! Embrace!

Solomon does that to get across to us that what he's saying is both *urgent* (he wants us to do something) and *practical* (he's telling us what he wants us to do). He gives us three things that the son is to **be** if he is to get wisdom in order to guard his heart.

1. **The son is to be a student — his heart must be educated (vv. 1-5)**
   In these verses we get lots of words like:
   Instruction, understanding, sound learning, teaching; words, commands, wisdom.

Getting wisdom into our hearts begins by learning from God's word. And for Solomon this is something that is to be happening continuously, not something that we do once. The day we stop getting educated is the day we stop being wise. Learning wisdom is not like the job of a painter, who can start painting a room, and pop out to a local café for a drink and a sandwich, and then return to the job to carry on. Learning wisdom is more like the job of a guy who's employed to push a boulder up a hill. If he takes a break to go for a drink and a sandwich, when he comes back he finds that the boulder is at the bottom of the hill again.

We need to keep at it. Constantly, always, and forever learning.

And don't think that just because we were awful at school and have no qualifications that this learning is beyond us. In Proverbs it's not so much about brains as decision – if you want it, come and get it.

2. **The son is to be a lover – his heart must be won (v. 6, 8)**

    Here the son is to go beyond learning to loving, beyond intellect to intimacy. The language here is actually a bit saucy. <u>Wisdom</u> is to be **loved**, **cherished**, and **embraced**. This is pillow talk. This is love-language. This is Barry White kind of stuff! This is where you want to shout, *'find a room!'* It reminds us that <u>wisdom in Proverbs is always relational</u>. It's **intimacy**, **closeness**, with the one who **protects**, **watches**, **guides**, and **leads** us.

Guarding our heart will mean coming to and knowing the one who will guard it for us.

It's a bit like celebrities that hire personal bodyguards. For them safety is found in sticking close to the person who will protect them. Guarding our heart will mean that we love, cherish, and embrace Jesus as the one who will guard our heart for us. We're like sheep who stick close to Jesus, knowing that He calls Himself the gate who protects us from those who would kill and destroy, and the shepherd who lays down His life for the sheep (**John 10:1-18**).

3. **The son is to be an investor – his heart must be undivided (v. 7)**

    Solomon knows that if the son is going to guard his heart it will mean hard choices and real sacrifices. Listen, my son: *'The beginning of wisdom is this: Get wisdom. Though it cost all you have, get understanding.'* We can tell by the choices someone makes what they consider to be *'above all else.'*

    If we consider outward appearance above all else, we'll sacrifice our health by not eating in order to have the 'perfect' body.

    If we consider our pleasure above all else, we'll steal from our own mother or teach our children to steal in order to feed our drug habit.

    If we consider our car above all else, we'll leech off our parents by living in their house till we're thirty-four so we can spend all our money blinging out our cars.

Likewise, we can tell by the choices someone makes whether they consider guarding their heart 'above all else.'

> The time they spend reading the Bible and praying.
> The lie-in's they forfeit in order to get to church.
> The old pals they walk away from to avoid bad influences.
> The freedom they give up in order to stay accountable.
> The alcohol they abstain from in order to be faithful to Jesus.
> The girlfriend they leave to walk in obedience to God's word.
> The TV in their bedroom they removed in order to remove temptation late at night.

It may cost all we have. But, listen to the words of Jesus in **Matthew 13:45-46**: 'Again, the kingdom of heaven is like a merchant looking for fine pearls. When he found one of great value, he went away and sold everything he had and bought it.'

 'What good will it be for someone to gain the whole world, yet forfeit their soul?' **Matthew 16:26**

The pearl is *worth* selling everything for. Gaining the world is *not* worth losing our soul.

So, to get wisdom in, the son is to be a **student**, a **lover**, and an **investor**.

GARY

Gary's problem is that he's never been very good at learning. He just finds it hard to take stuff in. He understands that we have to love God but what about loving yourself. He had a social worker once who told him he just had to 'love himself more.' Isn't he better looking after himself first and then worrying about God? And sometimes, you know, he feels that he should put his family before God and church. That's why he doesn't go every week. He takes his son to the footie. So, what would God prefer him to do? Go to a Sunday service or be a good dad?

STOP

Q: *What advice do you have for Gary based on what we've learned so far in this chapter?*

If the first part of guarding our heart is getting wisdom in, then the second part is **KEEPING WICKEDNESS OUT**.

3X *'Listen, my son, accept what I say, and the years of your life will be many. I instruct you in the way of wisdom and lead you along straight paths. When you walk, your steps will not be hampered; when you run, you will not stumble. Hold on to instruction, do not let it go; guard it well, for it is your life. Do not set foot on the path of the wicked or walk in the way of evildoers. Avoid it, do not travel on it; turn from it and go on your way. For they cannot rest until they do evil; they are robbed of sleep till they make someone stumble. They eat the bread of wickedness and drink the wine of violence. The path of the righteous is like the morning sun, shining ever brighter till the full light of day. But the way of the wicked is like deep darkness; they do not know what makes them stumble.'* **Proverbs 4:10-19**

Solomon gets the semi-automatic out again and showers us in a bunch of urgent and practical commands: *Don't set foot! Avoid! Don't travel on! Turn!* For Solomon there are only two paths in life:

The way of wisdom in **v. 11**.
The way of evildoers in **v. 14**.

The best way of guarding our heart, is <u>to keep far away from the way of evildoers</u>.

Wisdom is sometimes best expressed in <u>avoidance</u>.
Wisdom is sometimes most clearly demonstrated by extreme <u>separation</u>.

Guarding our heart will mean that:

there are places we don't go,
books we won't read;
magazines we don't buy,
fantasies we refuse to indulge,
friends we won't hang out with,
holidays we won't go on,
internet sites we won't click on.

We may think that that seems weak, or cowardly, or over-the-top, but for Solomon it is wise.

It would be foolish for a recovering alcoholic to wander into a pub.
It would be foolish for a recovering drug user to stroll into a drug den.
It would be foolish for a recovering sex addict to venture into a brothel.

We must not only avoid sin, but avoid the circumstances that would lead us to sin. For an alcoholic to walk into a pub, and then pray, *'Lord, lead me not into temptation,'* is like sticking our finger in a fire and then praying that it doesn't get burned!

The whole of the Bible is on the side of caution. We need to do all we can to keep wickedness out of our hearts. And sometimes that will mean running away like Joseph in **Genesis 39:12**. That's why in the New Testament over and over again we're commanded to 'Flee!' (**1 Cor. 6:18**; **1 Cor. 10:14**; **1 Tim. 6:11**; **2 Tim. 2:22**).

We take our heart with us wherever our feet go.
Our heart hears everything our ears listen to.
Our heart is exposed to everything our eyes see.

So guarding our heart will often mean **not going**, **not listening**, and **not seeing**. Guard it!

3X *'Blessed is the one who does not walk in step with the wicked or stand in the way that sinners take or sit in the company of mockers...'* **Psalms 1:1**

Did you notice the subtle slowing down of this guy? First, he's <u>walking in step with them</u> – he's just seeing what they're up to. Then, <u>he's standing with them</u> – he's listening to what they've got to say. All of a sudden, <u>he's taken a seat</u> – he's at home and comfortable with them.

He got too *close*. He was too *casual*. And now he's too *comfy* to get out. The lesson? *Don't set foot! Avoid! Don't travel on! Turn back!*

GARY

So you're saying I can't hang out with family and friends? I can't go down the pub?

STOP

Q: *Is that what we're saying? If not, how would you help decide what would be a wise decision to make in these circumstances?*

 MEMORY VERSE

'Above all else, guard your heart, for everything you do flows from it.'
Proverbs 4:23

 SUMMARY

Gary, listen, my son. Everything you do flows from your heart. So above all else, guard it by doing everything possible to get wisdom in, and everything possible to keep wickedness out. There will be some things to love and study, and other things to run away from.

WHAT'S THE POINT?

TEMPTATION IS LIKE A PROSTITUTE WHO OFFERS YOU A GOOD TIME BUT ENDS UP KILLING YOU.

SIX:
WHO AM I SLEEPING WITH?

GARY

Gary knows what it is to cheat on his partner. He has done it numerous times over the years. Many of them have been one night stands and at other times he has moved out of their home but never for more than six months at a time. Even though he is now a Christian he is still battling his sin and many of the women he has slept with keep in touch with him through social media. He's constantly getting invitations to meet up with them in secret. What harm would it do right? Everybody does it. Well, all his mates anyway. What should he do?

At some point in our lives most of us will have gone through a messy relationship break-up. But the mother of all messes usually comes when the break-up was down to one person in the relationship cheating on the other. When that happens, the person cheated on rightly feels betrayed, wounded, and livid as promises have been broken and trust has been exploited.

In a marriage we'd call it adultery.

In Proverbs already Solomon's introduced us to Woman Wisdom. She is a picture of God's wisdom. In fact, she's a preview of Jesus who, Paul tells us in **Colossians 2:3**, is the one, *'in whom are hidden all the treasures of wisdom and knowledge'.*

If we're to have another woman in our life, then we better make sure her name is *wisdom*. She's the one we should listen to. And from Proverbs 5, she's the one we're to be intimate with – *love, cherish, embrace*. And this is no open-relationship. It's to be exclusive.

But Woman Wisdom is not the only girl who's whispering in our ears seeking our attention.

> There's another voice.
> There's another woman.

And in Proverbs 5 she's sexting us, trying to allure and seduce us. Solomon is using this picture language to warn his son.

> Temptation to sin is powerful because it's **seductive** – <u>it looks amazing</u>.
> But engaging in sin is serious because it's **adulterous** – <u>it's like cheating</u>.

> > **Sin** is like a fling with another girl.
> > **Sin** is adultery against God.

It's giving our time, our energy, our love and our emotions to something other than God. Solomon wants us to take all the experience and emotions that we've witnessed or felt ourselves when someone has an affair, and map it on to our relationship with God when we sin against him.

3X *'My son, pay attention to my wisdom, turn your ear to my words of insight, that you may maintain discretion and your lips may preserve knowledge. For the lips of the adulterous woman* **drip honey***, and her speech is* **smoother than oil***....'* **Proverbs 5:1-3**

Gary, like all of us, needs to be on the lookout for, *'the adulterous woman.'*

Usually when men want to describe a beautiful woman they will start with her features. They will describe her body or her eyes or the way she talks and walks. But not Solomon. He doesn't warn his son to be on the lookout for a sexy stunner. He doesn't tell us her body measurements, what she's wearing or how she smells. That's where the stimulation usually lies right?

But, instead, he goes straight for <u>what she says</u>. He concentrates on <u>her words</u>. Why? Who measures the beauty and seductiveness of a woman by what she says? It's because Solomon knows that all seduction and temptation and sin are not actually aimed at our eyes, but seeks **to capture our hearts**.

It's always a story that our hearts crave and believe. So, take staring at a stripper on our computer screen, we're always telling our heart a story:

> *'I deserve this for all the hard work I've done recently.'*
> *'I'm taking revenge for the fact my wife doesn't satisfy me.'*
> *'This will help you medicate your negative feelings about yourself.'*
> *'With this you can be in control without having to be vulnerable.'*
> *'This person accepts me as I am, without being compared to anyone else.'*

<u>There's always a story that our hearts are craving</u>.

And so Solomon concentrates on the words that would capture our hearts. And he says they are words that,

> *'drip honey'*
> and are
> *'smoother than oil.'*

> **They go down easy.**
> **They're sweet.**
> **They appear harmless.**

But, <u>all is not what it seems</u>.

3X *...**but in the end** she is bitter as gall, sharp as a double-edged sword. Her feet go down to death; her steps lead straight to the grave. She gives no thought to the way of life; her paths wander aimlessly, but she does not know it. Now then, my sons, listen to me; do not turn aside from what I say. Keep to a path far from her, do not go near the door of her house, lest* *you lose your honour to others and your dignity to one who is cruel, lest strangers feast on your wealth and your toil enrich the house of another.* **At the end** *of your life you will groan, when your flesh and body are spent. You will say, 'How I hated discipline! How my heart spurned correction! I would not obey my teachers or turn my ear to my instructors. And I was soon in serious trouble in the assembly of God's people.'* **Proverbs 5:4-14**

Normally, when someone gives away the ending of a story or a movie they totally spoil it for us and we feel like smacking them across the face. But here Solomon is desperate for his son to find out what happens *'in the end'* (**v. 4**) and *'at the end'* (**v. 11**). He says, *'Listen, my son. Let me fast-forward to the end of the story and give away what happens.'*

Get past the sweetness.
Look beyond the smoothness.
See where her lips and her words will take you...

In the end the sweetness has turned to bitterness.
In the end the smoothness has changed to sharpness.

What **starts off as delicious** ends up as disgusting.
What **starts off as lovely** ends up as lethal.

She may have sweet lips,
but her feet go down to death,
and her steps lead to the grave.

The power of temptation is in hiding this *'end'* from you.

Foolishness is living only for the moment, and forgetting the consequences.

At the end of our life, if we live like this, listening to and loving the voice of the adulterous woman, we will *'groan when our flesh and body are spent.'* Solomon says to his son,

'Listen, my son.'

'See past the delusional young dreamer excited about the next high and the next time he gets laid, and see the creepy old man who has wasted his life and spent his soul on stuff that robbed him of everything.'

'See past the short-lived satisfaction of pornography and see the unsatisfied, guilt-laden woman who's real-life sexual experiences have never lived up to the fantasy-fiction she portrays on the internet.'

'See past the smiling face of the young lad peer-pressured into smoking weed for the first time who's enjoying being one of the boys, and see the lonely, frail, toothless old man whose family are ashamed of him and whose kids want nothing to do with him.'

Four times in **verses 12-14** this man condemns himself, letting out a low growl of pain and grief.

> **He's not satisfied**, he's spent.
> **He's not rejoicing**, he's ruined.

And as Solomon *fast-forwards* so that his son can see the end he's warning him that there is no *rewind*. And he's pleading with him not to waste his life living for what will never, ever, satisfy.

> The voice of this woman will promise us much, but deliver nothing.
> She'll promise to make us full, but she'll leave us empty.
> She'll promise a thrill, but leave us feeling guilty.
> She'll promise us freedom, but leave us enslaved.
> She'll promise us love, but she'll leave us lonely.
> She'll promise us life, but she'll lead us to the grave.

GARY

Since he's become a Christian Gary has stopped cheating on his partner. Instead, he's been 'sticking to porn', he tells you proudly. In his mind that is not bad. He's not hurting anybody and he's not being a cheat.

STOP

Q: *What do you say to Gary about this? How might Proverbs 5 help him to think this through more clearly?*

 'For your ways are in full view of the Lord, and he examines all your paths. The evil deeds of the wicked ensnare them; the cords of their sins hold them fast. For lack of discipline they will die, led astray by their own great folly.'
Proverbs 5:21-23

Gary needs to understand that in the moment of temptation one of the first **lies** we believe is that <u>no-one will see what we're doing</u>. Indeed, often in the moment immediately before we sin, the last thought that goes through our mind is that <u>we'll get away with it</u>. As we look back over our lives there are probably a few things that we have managed to hide from our partners and our kids or from our family. Some of us have tried to live a double-life to hide an addiction or an affair or whatever.

In these things <u>secrecy is our best friend</u> and <u>exposure our worst nightmare</u>.

The verses above remind us that we might be able to hide it from everyone else – maybe even deceiving ourselves – but **we can never hide anything from God**.

> Our ways are in His *full view*.
>> And He doesn't just see them.
> He examines them. *All* of them.

 ILLUSTRATION

Imagine if we wait until our wife/husband is out of the house and we invite somebody around with the sole intention of cheating. We take them into the bedroom and close the door. Now if that was not bad enough, imagine doing the same thing with our husband/wife in the bedroom standing in the corner watching us.

That is what is happening when we sin. We may well be doing it in secret from loved ones but **the Lord sees everything we do all of the time**.

<u>Sin is cheating on God with another person</u> – **while He is in the room!**

Maybe we don't think our sin is that bad. Maybe we think we've lived a good life, we just haven't thought much about God until this point. Well, even still, if this was <u>the</u> relationship we were created for, then the offence of absence is just as bad as the offence of adultery. Imagine a relationship where one partner lived their life without ever relating to or speaking to the other partner! Either way, God has a right to be as betrayed, wounded and angry as we would be when cheated on or ignored.

The day I wrote this chapter Muhammad Ali, the world-famous boxer died. Everyone's talking about him. Social media is full of tributes. But one guy I read made an interesting comment. He said, *'the greatest fighter of them all was brought down because of the fight that he so loved.'*

The thing he loved took his life.

A career in boxing where he took constant knocks to his temple was a significant factor in his death. That's very like our sin. <u>The thing we love the most, is the thing that takes our life away</u>.

GARY

Gary's been involved in a one-to-one discipleship relationship with a more mature Christian man from his church. Every week Gary gets asked lots of questions about his walk with Jesus, including how his ongoing battle with lust and pornography is. For the last few months Gary's been lying in his one-to-one, saying that he's not been tempted in that area for a while. The truth is, Gary's fallen back into a recurring pattern of looking at porn when his partner has already gone to bed.

STOP
Q: What would you say to Gary from Proverbs 5 to help him be honest with his accountability partner?

What's amazing in all of this is, that

> when we loved our sin, it actually took life away from us,
> > but when God has every reason to take our life away because of our sin, He loves us still.

Even when our adultery is in full view, He loves us!

Romans 5:6-11 explains that when we were *powerless* Christ died for the ungodly.

But we weren't just *powerless*. It says that when we were still *sinners*, Christ died for us.
But we weren't just *powerless sinners*. It says that when we were His *enemies*, God saved us.

Even when I was a **powerless**, **sinful**, **enemy** of God, <u>He loved me and sent His son to die for me</u>.

This is where real change begins: remembering that the voice of temptation that offers me life *in the end* will take my life; and remembering that the voice of wisdom offers me life *even when* I deserve death, and so we begin to love God more than our sin.

 MEMORY VERSE
'For your ways are in full view of the Lord, and he examines all your paths.'
Proverbs 5:21

SUMMARY

Gary, listen, my son. Temptation is a whore who will do anything to get you into bed with her. She looks amazing, and says all the right things. But beware: she promises life, but she'll bring you to the grave.

WHAT'S THE POINT?

BECAUSE WE SIN IN EVERY AREA OF LIFE, GOD GIVES US WISDOM FOR EVERY AREA OF LIFE.

SEVEN:
HOW DO I ESCAPE?

RECAP

Every Christian needs God's wisdom to live for Jesus in this world.
The path we walk in life is full of hidden traps.
God has got our backs and will protect us if we listen and obey His voice.
We must trust God and not our own understanding if we want to get by
*   in life.*
Guard your heart above all other things.
Temptation is like a prostitute who promises you a good time but ends up
*   killing you.*

What did you do yesterday?

The chances are that it was pretty similar to what you did the day before, and the day before that, and the day before that. There are some big, exciting moments in life that stand out – weddings, parties, babies, sporting finals... But often life is just normal, regular, mundane routine.

For Solomon, that's exactly where the battle between voices occurs. That's exactly where the choices between Woman Wisdom's voice and the Adulterous Woman's voice are going to be made.

> *In the normal, regular, mundane routines of life.*
> > *We need the gospel in every area of life because we sin in every*
> > *area of life.*

In this bit of Proverbs Solomon takes his son to three areas of everyday life and applies the voice of wisdom to it. Think of Solomon a bit like the ghosts of Christmas Past, Present, and Yet to Come in *The Muppet Christmas*

Carol. He takes his son to various situations to help him learn important lessons that will affect the course of his life. Or think of these three things like the boss you have to fight at the end of a level on a platform game on your console – like Bebop and Rocksteady or Donkey Kong (google them if you have no idea what I'm talking about!). The enemies that the son will comes up against every day, according to Proverbs, are **the hunter, the bandit**, and **the villain**.

THE HUNTER | The Son Who's Ensnared

3X *'My son, if you have put up security for your neighbour, if you have shaken hands in pledge for a stranger, you have been trapped by what you said, ensnared by the words of your mouth. So do this, my son, to free yourself, since you have fallen into your neighbour's hands: go – to the point of exhaustion – and give your neighbour no rest! Allow no sleep to your eyes, no slumber to your eyelids. Free yourself, like a gazelle from the hand of the hunter, like a bird from the snare of the fowler.'* **Proverbs 6:1-5**

Solomon's son finds himself ensnared like a bird caught in a trap. How? The situation seems to be:

> *One of his neighbours was strapped for cash, so they apply for a loan.*
> *The lender wants a security guarantee on his money.*
> *Solomon's son agrees to be the guarantor who will pay if his neighbour can't.*

We don't know why the son agrees to do it. Maybe he was just being nice. Maybe he thought it was possibly a way to make a quick profit. We don't know. All we know is, the debtor failed on his payments, and so the lender's knocking on the son's door wanting his money, and threatening to send the heavies round if he doesn't produce the cash. He's found himself

Trapped
Ensnared

Solomon is desperate to get some financial wisdom into his son's head. Listen, my son:

You can be generous and yet be foolish.
You can be nice and yet get stung for it.
You can try to be helpful, and yet end up hurting yourself and the person you tried to help.

Money can be a great servant when you're wise with it,
but it's a terrible master if you're foolish with it.

How many of us have taken out an impulsive loan to get something we really wanted, and then lived trapped and ensnared by the ridiculously high interest rates on the repayment? **We were so fixated on the £ signs that we were blind to the % signs**.

How many of us have wildly overspent on our kids' Christmas presents, wanting to keep up with what our pals are getting their kids, only to find that we're trapped by the payments six months later? **And the irony is our kids don't even thank us because they think they're from Santa.**

The adulterous woman will make us concentrate on the bigger TV we can get **now**, or the holiday we can have **now**, or the dog we can have **now**, or the popularity we could have **now**. And she'll blind us to the debt that will come later.

Whether it's spending or saving, lending or borrowing, the questions we need to ask ourselves are: Is this:

wise or foolish?
prudent or impulsive?
generous or selfish?
evidence that I'm serving God or evidence that money is my master?
helping the person I'm giving this to or will it only help them continue a lifestyle they can't afford?

<u>He's not saying don't be generous</u>. He's just saying be wise about it. Don't rush into it and then get trapped and remove your ability to be generous again. And don't rush into it and then get stung by a bad experience that will remove your willingness to be generous again.

<u>Be wise</u>.

And if the son's been foolish, Solomon says: Listen, my son,

> *free yourself; go — to the point of exhaustion; give your neighbour no rest; allow no sleep to your eyes; free yourself!*

He recommends energetic, costly, urgent action to get out of this trap.

If our past life has left us ensnared by money issues, we should do everything we can **right now** to get ourselves out of them. **Don't ignore them** and try to run from them.

<u>Be wise</u>.

We should get all the help we can from our church and/or from a mature Christian. And work towards our freedom.

GARY

Gary's always considered himself to be pretty savvy with his money. He and the family have always lived pretty much hand-to-mouth, but they've always 'got by'. When things have been tight or his kid's birthday's come round he's always managed to cut a deal or borrow from a pal. Since becoming a Christian his mentor at church has helped him put together a monthly budget to help him organise his money. But this week his car broke down and there's a hefty bill to pay that is nowhere close to being in his budget. He's seen an advert for a quick-loan on TV. It said something about interest on repayments, but not understanding what it meant he's thinking about just going for it.

STOP

Q: If you were his mentor, what advice would you give Gary having just read **Proverbs 6:1-5?**

THE BANDIT | The Sluggard Who Sleeps

3X *'Go to the ant, you sluggard; consider its ways and be wise! It has no commander, no overseer or ruler, yet it stores its provisions in summer and gathers its food at harvest. How long will you lie there, you sluggard? When will you get up from your sleep? A little sleep, a little slumber, a little folding of the hands to rest – and poverty will come on you like a thief and scarcity like an armed man.'* **Proverbs 6:6-11**

Meet the sluggard.

He's a lazy, good-for-nothing bum.

He's the bloke in **Proverbs 26:15** who *'buries his hand in the dish; he is too lazy to bring it back to his mouth'.* If someone's so lazy that they stick a fork in a bowl of chips and then can't be bothered to bring it to their mouth, then they've definitely got issues!

The trouble is, in our culture the sluggard is hailed as a hero or a role model to be admired and imitated. **Hard work is like a contagious disease to be avoided at all costs**. And our sofas are like a life support machine that we never want to be too far away from.

Solomon stands the sluggard next to the ant, and makes a brutal comparison.

> **The ant has no commander**, but you have the voice of Wisdom.
> **The ant has no overseer**, but you have a Lord who examines all your ways.
> **The ant has no ruler**, but you have a God to whom you'll have to give an account for your life.

In Solomon's day, if you didn't work, you didn't eat. So if you were too lazy to work, it wasn't just a case of falling comfortably onto the government's security system. If you didn't work, you starved. But the sluggard is so foolish he doesn't realise that the life-support-machine of his sofa is more of a death-trap. In the New Testament laziness isn't just physically foolish, it's spiritually wicked.

Jesus is black and white on the issue:

No one has <u>ever</u> been lazy and faithful to God (**Matt. 25:26**).

Paul is black and white on the issue:

Laziness denies the gospel – God saved you by grace and now has good works prepared for you to do (**Eph. 2:8-10**).

Laziness puts off outsiders – whereas hard work will win the respect of those outside the church (**1 Thess. 4:11-12**).

Laziness burdens the church (**2 Thess. 3:7-10**).

Laziness means you can't help those in need (**Eph. 4:28**).

If this is you, Solomon asks you, *'How long will you lie there…? When will you get up from your sleep?'* It's already been too long. Today you need to listen to God's voice saying *'Wake up! Get up! Stop being a fool! It's time to start being a good and faithful servant of Jesus* (**Matt. 25:21, 23**).

GARY

Gary's achieved a huge amount of things in his life. He's conquered kingdoms. He's won World Championships. He's defeated evil villains. He's built worldwide empires. He's overthrown drug-lords. He's even been into space. The thing is, they've all been in a fantasy world on his games console. He's proud of his achievements. But, in the cold light of day, in real life all he's done is sat on a chair and twiddled his thumbs for days and weeks on end. In the real world, he's truly lazy. He can give the impression that he's working hard, but he only does it when someone's eye is on him.

STOP

Q: What would you say to Gary from what we've seen in Proverbs 6? Look also at **Ephesians 5:8-17** and **Ephesians 6:5-8**.

THE VILLAIN | The Scoundrel Who Stirs

 'A troublemaker and **a villain**, who goes about with a corrupt mouth, who winks maliciously with his eye, signals with his feet and motions with his fingers, who plots evil with deceit in his heart — he always stirs up conflict. Therefore, disaster will overtake him in an instant; he will suddenly be destroyed — without remedy. There are six things the Lord hates, seven that are detestable to him: haughty eyes, a lying tongue, hands that shed innocent blood, a heart that devises wicked schemes, feet that are quick to rush into evil, a false witness who pours out lies and a person who stirs up conflict in the community.' **Proverbs 6:12-19**

Solomon switches from sinful idleness in the sluggard to <u>sinful busyness in the scoundrel</u>.

Here's a person who, from

> top to bottom,
> > inside to outside,
> > > from relationship to God to relationship to their community
> **is nothing but trouble**.

As Solomon describes this person what smacks us in the face is that they are all so *normal*. They are all so *me*. It's back to where we started when we talked about the normal, regular, mundane routines of life.

<u>Dodgy deals; thinking the worst of people; plotting against people; deliberately provoking people; thinking too highly of myself; telling lies; hurting people; stirring up conflict.</u>

I know I've done most of those things already *today*.

And yet it's these things that we are told God *hates* and *detests*. So if you follow the logic, then if it's these things God hates, and if these things are my things, then because of my sin **I am an object of God's hatred**.

Ouch.

Now, before we go off on a line of thought that says, *'If God is a God of hatred then I want nothing to do with Him. The God I like to think of is a God of love...'*, think about it. God has every right to hate those who sin. It is because of our sin that Jesus, the Son of God, had to die.

If it was my son who was on the other end of these things, if my son was the one who was plotted against, deliberately provoked, told lies, hurt horribly by others, and thrown into the midst of conflict, how would you expect me to react? If I was unmoved, passive, and didn't care that my son was being targeted and abused, would you say I was a loving parent?

No.

You'd expect me to be full of rage. You'd expect me to want to protect my child. You'd expect me to want justice. You'd expect me to want to put an end to the evil behaviour.

God is a God of love. But He is also a **God of justice** who cares deeply when His people are harmed by the actions and sins of others. <u>It is a good thing</u> that **God hates and detests lying**. It is a good thing that **God hates and detests those who kill the innocent**.

> *We do want a God who is against these kinds of things.*
> *We do want a God who will get rid of all evil and wickedness.*

<u>Our problem</u> is, He is also a **God who is against us**.
<u>Our problem</u> is, He is a **God who rightly could get rid of us**.

The good news of the Bible is that although we **ought** to be an object of God's wrath who **ought** to be destroyed, God looks on us with <u>underserved kindness</u> as an object of His **mercy**. <u>God sends Jesus to become an object of God's hatred who on the cross is destroyed instead of us</u>. Jesus enters the day of disaster to suffer hell, that we might enter unending days of joy in God's New Creation.

This is the story we need to hear.
This is the voice we need to listen to.

So that as we clearly see the mind-blowing, costly, love of God, we are going to love Him so much that we no longer want to be busy doing the things that He hates, but long to get busy doing the things that make Him smile.

⚒ MEMORY VERSE

'There are six things the Lord hates, seven that are detestable to him: haughty eyes, a lying tongue, hands that shed innocent blood, a heart that devises wicked schemes, feet that are quick to rush into evil, a false witness who pours out lies and a person who stirs up conflict in the community.'
Proverbs 6:16-19

📍 SUMMARY

Gary, listen, my son. Life is sometimes dull and boring. Your life will be made up of the normal, regular, and the mundane. But that's exactly where the choices between wisdom and foolishness are going to be made. You'll need God's wisdom in every area of life because you'll be tempted to sin in every area of your life.

WHAT'S THE POINT?

WE NEED TO LEARN TO SAY 'NO' TO SIN OVER AND OVER, AND TO KEEP LEARNING ABOUT THE DANGERS OF SIN OVER AND OVER.

EIGHT:
WHAT IF I'VE BEEN A
FOOL ... AGAIN?

GARY

Gary is feeling discouraged yet again. He feels like he is winning in one area of his life when it comes to temptation and then something else pops up. Then, out of the blue, a sin he thought he had beaten comes back around again. What is going on? His head is spinning.

Reading **Proverbs 6:20–7:27** feels like the movie *Groundhog Day*. We immediately get the feeling like we're stuck in a time-loop going round and round, repeating the same thing over and over. Because once again we're back hearing the voice of the Adulterous Woman.

Don't forget what we noticed earlier on in the book:

Repetition is the key to education.
Repetition is the key to education.
Repetition is the key to education.

It's a reminder to Gary, and to all of us, that the fight to walk on the path of wisdom is a fight to be fought every single day. The Adulterous Woman is a stubborn old mare who will **keep coming back**. Saying 'no' once is not enough. We need to be ready to say 'no' to the voice of temptation multiple times every day.

We may have read Proverbs a few times by now.
We may have made promises to God that we will not sin again.

But.

More than likely <u>we will have fallen back into old sinful patterns</u> if we've taken our eye off the Lord, even if only for a moment. That's why Solomon says *'Let's go round again...'*

Solomon knows that wisdom will be like a light to his son guiding him along a safe path. Solomon knows that just as you can't scoop fire into your lap without getting burned so you can't walk on the path of foolishness without falling into sin. So he sits his son down at the window of his house and he tells his son a story.

It's a story about a fool.

He wants his son to learn from the fool's mistakes from the safety of his window, so that he doesn't make the same mistakes. His son is not a fool.

Not yet anyway.

And Solomon tells this story to stop him from becoming one.

3X *'At the window of my house I looked down through the lattice. I saw among the simple, I noticed among the young men, a youth who had no sense. He was going down the street near her corner, walking along in the direction of her house at twilight, as the day was fading, as the dark of night set in. Then out came a woman to meet him, dressed like a prostitute and with crafty intent. (She is unruly and defiant, her feet never stay at home; now in the street, now in the squares, at every corner she lurks.) She took hold of him and kissed him and with a brazen face she said: "Today I fulfilled my vows, and I have food from my fellowship offering at home. So I came out to meet you; I looked for you and have found you! I have covered my bed with coloured linens from Egypt. I have perfumed my bed with myrrh, aloes and cinnamon. Come, let's drink deeply of love till morning; let's enjoy ourselves with love! My husband is not at home; he has gone on a long journey. He took his purse filled with money and will not be home till full moon." With persuasive words she led him astray; she seduced him with her smooth talk. All at once he followed her like an ox going to the slaughter, like a deer stepping into a noose till an arrow pierces his liver, like a bird* *darting into a snare, little knowing it will cost him his life. Now then, my sons, listen to me; pay attention to what I say. Do not let your heart turn to her ways or stray into her paths. Many are the victims she has brought down; her slain are a mighty throng. Her house is a highway to the grave, leading down to the chambers of death.'* **Proverbs 7:6-23**

Imagine this story was a sporting event and you were the pundit in the TV studio after the game, picking apart the highlights and pointing out where this young man made mistakes and where the adulterous woman was clever in her offence.

Let's look first at the young lad...

'NO SENSE'

V7 describes him as *'a youth who had no sense.'* Time and time again Proverbs has told us to **get wisdom, get wisdom, get wisdom**. It's commanded us to **be on guard**. This lad has done neither. He was simple and had no sense. Life is too dangerous to lack sense. Walking through life with no sense is like wandering on to a battlefield completely unarmed and minus your body armour. No man's land is no place for a stroll!

'NEAR'

V8 says that he was *'going down the street near her corner.'* The repeated command of Solomon has been to **flee sin**, not flirt with it. But this young man, lacking sense, walks near to the Adulterous Woman's territory.
Temptation is like a magnet.
The nearer you get the harder it is to walk away.
To be *near it* is to be naive.

'TWILIGHT'

V9 emphasizes three times what time of day it was, he was *'walking along in the direction of her house at twilight, as the day was fading, as the dark of night set in.'* Taking that at face value, it's true that often our worst moments happen in the dark. It's why night clubs happen at night. It's why drug deals go down late at night. It's why people lie in their beds at night plotting revenge or indulging sexual fantasies.

<u>We need to be especially on our guard against temptation to sin at night</u>.

But it's also a picture. Darkness in the Bible is often imagery for danger or sinful behaviour (**1 Thess. 5:4-11**). This young man is swaggering happily into the underworld that rebels against the God of Light, wrongly presuming that the cover of darkness hides his sin from God's sight.

We could add at this point that he's not only lacking sense, at the wrong place, at the wrong time, but he's also alone. He's isolated. That's always dangerous and foolish when trying to battle sin. Solitude and shallow relationships are Satan's allies in temptation.

<u>Community and deep relationships are great weapons against Satan's schemes</u>.

GARY

Gary finds that the battle against sin is hardest at night. It seems that all his Christian pals are heading to bed just when his non-Christian pals are about to get out and have a good time. It's the time of day when he feels the strongest draw back to his old lifestyle. It's the time of day when he gets the most texts from his pals telling him to come round for a few beers.

STOP

Q: *What can Gary learn from this young man's story that will help him make wise decisions?*

At this point, let's move to examine the Adulterous Woman's offensive tactics...

In **verse 10** she comes out to meet him. **James 4:7** says that *if you resist the devil he'll flee from you*. But this shows us that <u>if we take one step in his direction he'll take ten towards us</u>. This woman doesn't come out to him all timid and shy. She doesn't play hard to get. Immediately she assaults and overwhelms every one of his senses:

She thrills *his eyes with what she wears* (**v. 10**)
She intoxicates *him through touch* (**v. 13**)
She indulges *his taste with the offer of food* (**v. 14**)
She dominates *his ears with her words* (**vv. 14-21**)
She stimulates *his sense of smell* (**v. 17**)

<u>She assaults all of his senses to capture his heart.</u>

But look closely at her words. She says, *'My husband is not at home; he has gone on a long journey. He took his purse filled with money and will not be home till full moon.'* With persuasive words she led him astray; she seduced him with her smooth talk.

She doesn't even try and convince him that it's right, <u>only that they'll get away with it</u>.

Now, come back to the young lad and let's highlight his final two mistakes...

SILENT LISTENING

If we read back through the whole story, we'll notice that through the whole thing the son doesn't say a single word. Not one word.

He's completely passive.
He doesn't ask her to leave him alone.
He doesn't tell her to shut-up.
He doesn't question her words.
He doesn't combat her lies with truth.
He doesn't challenge her foolishness with wisdom.

Instead, like a gullible, stupid fish he bites down on the bait fully aware that it hides a dirty big hook.

I heard an old saying somewhere that said, *'You can't stop a bird from flying over your head but you can stop it from making a nest in your hair.'* Applying that to this: we can't always stop temptation from flying over our head, but we can take action to make sure sin doesn't make a nest in our heart.

The young man's silence teaches Solomon's son to be vocal in the fight against sin.

When it lies, **speak God's truth** back at it.

Whenever you hear it, **pray and ask God** to help out.

When it's loud, **recite Scripture** louder.

When it looks so tempting, speak to your soul and **remind yourself** of its deadly end.

When you feel like giving in, **remind yourself of the gospel**.

GARY

One of the first memory verses Gary's pastor gave him was **Psalm 119:9-11**:

'How can a young person stay on the path of purity? By living according to your word. I seek you with all my heart; do not let me stray from your commands. I have hidden your word in my heart that I might not sin against you.'

STOP

Q: How does this verse explain how Gary should respond when the voice of temptation is loud in his ears?

DEADLY FOLLOWING

This is no *'and they all lived happily ever after'* story. Every one of his son's senses is seduced. And every one of his senses begins to worship her. But in **verses 22-23** we read, *'All at once he followed her like an ox going to the slaughter, like a deer stepping into a noose till an arrow pierces his liver, like a bird darting into a snare, little knowing it will cost him his life.'*

It's sadly simple:

he follows her;
she kills him.

Now, remember what she promised him: food on the table; beautiful Egyptian linen on the bed; stunning smells of myrrh, aloes, and cinnamon; sex all night long. What do you think he found when he followed her into her home? Here's my guess:

No food, no fancy linen, no beautiful smells, not even any sex.

Why?

Temptation <u>never provides what it promises</u>.
It <u>always lies</u>.
It <u>never presents itself with its true end in sight</u>.

Instead what did he find? **Verses 26-27** tell us, *'Many are the victims she has brought down; her slain are a mighty throng. Her house is a highway to the grave, leading down to the chambers of death.'*

'Listen, my son. Her bedroom is a cemetery. It's full of the skeletons of her many victims.'

Solomon is desperate for his son to learn from this man's mistakes. He's desperate for him to see the little decisions, the apparently trivial choices, made in the pattern of a very normal day – like walking down a street – can have a huge effect on the course of our life.

He wants his son to know that on the one hand we have an enemy who will come out to attack us, but on the other hand sometimes we are our own worst enemy with the choices we make. That's an important balance to remember. At the same time, we can be sinners and sufferers, fools and victims, self-harming and at the same time murdered. We need to be responsible and wise ourselves, whilst being aware and on guard against our enemy. There's no good news at the end of this chapter. Solomon ends the story there. He wants us to go away feeling the full force of his final words: *'Her house is a highway to the grave, leading down to the chambers of death.'*

MEMORY VERSE

'My son, keep my words and store up my commands within you. Keep my commands and you will live; guard my teachings as the apple of your eye.'
Proverbs 7:1-2

 SUMMARY

Gary, listen, my son. The adulterous woman is back again. Truth is you'll need to fight this battle every single day. Saying 'no' once is not enough. You need to be ready to say 'no' to her multiple times a day. And the little decisions, the apparently trivial choices, made in the pattern of a very normal day, will have a huge effect on the course of your life.

WHAT'S THE POINT?

TO TRULY BELIEVE IN JESUS MEANS THERE'S AN OLD WAY TO LEAVE AND A NEW WAY TO LIVE, AN INVITATION TO REJECT AND AN INVITATION TO ACCEPT.

NINE:
WHO WILL I SAY 'YES' TO?

RECAP

Every Christian needs God's wisdom to live for Jesus in this world.

The path we walk in life is full of hidden traps.

God has got our backs and will protect us if we listen and obey His voice.

We must trust God and not our own understanding if we want to get by in life.

Guard your heart above all other things.

Temptation is like a prostitute who promises you a good time but ends up killing you.

Because we need God's wisdom for every area of life.

We must learn to say 'no' to sin over and over.

STOP

Q: *Imagine I gave you the opportunity to have a meal at your favourite restaurant, with seven other people of your choice. They could be anyone, dead or alive – family, celebrities, movie characters, cartoons, sports stars. Which seven people would you invite?*

Who we'd invite to that meal would reveal a lot about us. It would reveal our interests. It might reveal what decade we grew up in. It might reveal that we love to laugh. It might reveal that we value family. It might reveal that we've got terrible taste in music. We'll come back to that...

There was a Guinness advert a few years ago that had the tag line: *'The choices we make reveal the true nature of our character.'* That's very Proverbs. **The true nature of our character** – whether we are <u>wise</u> or whether we are a <u>fool</u> – **will be revealed in the choices we make**.

In Proverbs 9 Solomon allows <u>Woman Wisdom</u> and the <u>Adulterous Woman</u> one more chance to speak to his son. For these two women it's like this is their final song in the *Britain's Got Talent* final. They've got one shot. They're singing in the judges' vote off. This is their big finish. This is their last chance. And the son has got to cast his vote. Which woman will he choose?

Solomon knows that the choice he makes will reveal the true nature of his character...

3X *'Wisdom has built her house; she has set up its seven pillars. She has prepared her meat and mixed her wine; she has also set her table. She has sent out her servants, and she calls from the highest point of the city, "Let all who are simple come to my house!" To those who have no sense she says, "Come, eat my food and drink the wine I have mixed. Leave your simple ways and you will live; walk in the way of insight."'* **Proverbs 9:1-6**

WOMAN WISDOM'S BANQUET

Woman Wisdom is having a party. And here are the important details:

> The venue is at her house, which is a bit of a mansion (**v. 1**).
> The meal on offer is meat and wine – no veg, which is good news (**v. 2**).
> The table is prepared, set, and ready to go (**v. 2**).
> The Facebook event has been set up, and invitations sent out (**v. 3**).
> The location is at the highest point of the city (**v. 3**).

If we were to read the rest of the Old Testament, we would see similar language coming up elsewhere. So in **Isaiah 25:6** we read: *'On this mountain the Lord Almighty will prepare a feast of rich food for all peoples, a banquet of aged wine – the best of meats and the finest of wines.'* And in **Isaiah 55:1** we read: *'Come, all you who are thirsty, come to the waters; and you who have no money, come, buy and eat! Come, buy wine and milk without money and without cost. Why spend money on what is not bread, and your labour on what does not satisfy? Listen, listen to me, and eat what is good, and you will delight in the richest of fare.'*

Both of these tell us that in the Old Testament **God is the Great Host** of banquets like this one in Proverbs 9. More than that, **God is the Great Inviter** to such banquets. Woman Wisdom here stands in the place of God, with the voice of God, inviting us to the banquet in God's house.

That's why we're told that her house is at the highest point of the city, because in God's city, God's house – the temple – was at the highest point of that city. It's also why, when Jesus turns up in the gospels telling parables about banquets (**Luke 15:15-24**), He's not just telling nice stories, <u>He's claiming to **be** God</u>.

Anyway, back to Woman Wisdom. Who's invited to this banquet? **v. 4**, '*Let all who are [what] come in here.*'

> Does she say, '*Let all who are good and moral and righteous come in here'*?
> Does she say, '*Let all who are A-list or rich-list or royalty come in here'*?

There's a great host. It's a great banquet. Are they great guests?
Not so much.

She says, '*Let all who are simple come to my house!*' To those who have no sense she says, '*Come, eat my food and drink the wine I have mixed.*'

That language has come up before in Proverbs. **In Proverbs 7:6-7** we read, '*At the window of my house I looked down through the lattice. I saw among **the simple**, I noticed among the young men, a youth **who had no sense**.*' This simple guy who had no sense is the guy who jumps into bed with a whore. And *he's* invited to her banquet?! The guy who's still doing up his trousers as he comes out the brothel?! He's invited?!

How many of us invited this guy to our meal?

<u>The choices God makes reveal the true nature of His character</u>. And He invites *this* guy. God, the Great Host, the Great Inviter, reveals Himself to be a **gracious God**.

He invites people not on the basis of being worthy,
but on the basis of **His undeserved kindness**.
He invites people to what they don't deserve.

He invites the adulterer,
     the junkie,
          the sluggard,
               the glutton,
                    the murderer,
                         the fool,
                              the sinner.

'Let all who are simple come to my house!'

But notice *how* they are to come. **v. 6** says, *'Leave your simple ways and you will live; walk in the way of insight.'*

Leave and walk.

That's what the Bible calls repentance. <u>Leaving our old lifestyle</u>. And walking in a completely <u>new direction</u>. Being a Christian is not just about believing in Jesus.

     To truly believe in Jesus means
          there's an <u>old way to leave</u>,
               and <u>a new way to live</u>.

3X *'Whoever corrects a mocker invites insults; whoever rebukes the wicked incurs abuse. Do not rebuke mockers or they will hate you; rebuke the wise and they will love you. Instruct the wise and they will be wiser still; teach the righteous and they will add to their learning. The fear of the Lord is the beginning of wisdom, and knowledge of the Holy One is understanding. For through wisdom your days will be many, and years will be added to your life. If you are wise, your wisdom will reward you; if you are a mocker, you alone will suffer.'* **Proverbs 9:7-12**

THE RESPONSE TO WOMAN WISDOM

After she's sent out her invitation Woman Wisdom gets two very different responses. Some people mock her, insult her, abuse her, and hate her. Why? Well, when we call people *simple* who actually think they're *smart* then they're not going to like it. They'll respond by saying something like:

> 'How dare you say I'm simple and have no sense.'
> 'I'm not sitting at a banquet next to the sex-addict who's come straight from the brothel.'
> 'How dare you put me in the same category as him!'

It's an attitude that sticks their nose up in the air, and have their eyes looking down at everyone else. The invitation of Christianity is **first of all a confrontation**, because it's saying that you are simple, **you are a sinner**. And for some people that's reason enough to mock it and hate it. <u>If we are too proud to see and admit our faults and failings, we'll take the invitation as an insult</u>.

GARY

Gary's pastor has noticed that Gary is beginning to get a bit of an arrogant swagger around church. Another lad from the community has recently become a Christian, and because Gary's got more time under his belt, and he's no longer the newest Christian, he's starting to show off by using some of the Christian lingo he's learned. Also, he's not been responding well when challenged in his one-to-one about patterns of sin in his life. In his last discipleship meeting with his mentor he became very angry when he was asked about his attitude.

STOP

Q: Why is this a dangerous attitude for Gary to have? If he continues with this attitude where's it likely to lead him?

Some people mock wisdom. Some people, however, love her, and take the opportunity to become wiser and add to their learning. There are those who have a right view of themselves, who have a deep awareness of their sin and foolishness. And what makes the difference between these two groups of people is *'the fear of the Lord'* (**v. 10**). <u>When we're flat on our face in fear before God, we're in no position to look down our nose at anyone else</u>.

When Jesus walked the earth He got exactly the same split response. The stuck up, self-righteous people, hated Him, abused Him, and insulted Him. They hated the fact that He was always hanging around and eating with the dregs of society like tax collectors and sinners (**Matt. 9:11, Matt. 11:19**). But Jesus knew why He came. <u>He knew it was not the healthy who needed a doctor, but the sick</u>. And so He had come, not for the righteous but for sinners. For Jesus, the reason He dined with simple-sinners was because He was going to die for simple-sinners (**Matt. 26:28, John 6:56**). And those who knew themselves to be simple-sinners loved Him.

<u>We need to guard our heart against arrogance</u>. We need to **fear God** and **stay humble**. Don't ever think we deserve a seat at God's table. Don't ever think we've made it and have nothing more to learn.

<u>A wise believer is always</u>

> *teachable*
> *open to rebuke*
> *and eager to grow*

GARY
When Gary first became a Christian he really struggled with church. He had heard the good news that Jesus had come to die for sinners, and so he expected the church to feel like a hospital, where everyone was needy and broken like him. But when he walked in he felt like he was the only sinner in the room. It felt more like a fancy dinner party than a hospital ward. The culture of the church didn't seem to match the invitation of the gospel he'd received. People seemed to give the

impression that everything in their lives was 'fine' and that they had everything 'together.' Gary wanted to run straight back out the door.

STOP

Q: How can a church make people like Gary feel more welcome?

3✕ *'Folly is an unruly woman; she is simple and knows nothing. She sits at the door of her house, on a seat at the highest point of the city, calling out to those who pass by, who go straight on their way, "Let all who are simple come to my house!" To those who have no sense she says, "Stolen water is sweet; food eaten in secret is delicious!" But little do they know that the dead are there, that her guests are deep in the realm of the dead.'*
Proverbs 9:13-18

THE ADULTEROUS WOMAN'S BANQUET

As we've seen in Proverbs there's never just one voice. There's never just one invitation.

There's another woman (**v. 13**).
There's another house (**v. 14**).

But she's a rival at the same location – the highest point of the city (**v. 14**). And she's a rival to the same people (**v. 16**).

She says, *'Let all who are simple come to my house!'*

<u>Sin is no less eager to destroy us than wisdom is to save us</u>.

But look what she has to offer: *'Stolen water is sweet; food eaten in secret is delicious!'* Why on earth would the son choose stolen water over aged wine, and secret food over the best of meat? Because she appeals to the **twisted**, **warped**, **perverted** nature of our character that loves the short-lived adrenalin of doing something that we shouldn't. *One Republic* got this spot on in their lyrics:

'And I feel something so right by doing the wrong thing
And I feel something so wrong by doing the right thing
Everything that kills me makes me feel alive.'

 ILLUSTRATION

Imagine someone creating a video game for a console where we are rewarded for driving a car safely – observing the speed limits, being polite to pedestrians, observing all the laws of the road and parking neatly. No one would buy that game! But, create a game where we don't just drive, but we can steal cars, knock down pedestrians, buy guns, rob banks, rape women, and get chased by the police and we'll have ourselves a multi-million-pound business.

That's what the <u>Adulterous Woman</u> is appealing to.

But, again Solomon removes the bait to reveal the hook; he wants to prevent embarrassment by revealing the prank; he wants to save the animal's life by disarming the trap. There's always a 'but':

But little do they know that the dead are there,
that her guests are deep in the realm of the dead.'

Both women have sung their song. Both have given their invitations. Both stand arms outstretched, ready to welcome the son – and us – to a seat at their table.

Which voice are we listening to?
Which invitation are we accepting?
Which woman allures our heart?
Which feast excites our appetite?
Whose guest do we want to be?

The choices we make – every second of every day – will not only reveal the true nature of our character.

They will set the course of our life.
They will determine the place we spend eternity.

Jesus offers us a place at His table, to dine with Him for the rest of forever, even though our life reveals we've been simple and sinful. He raises His voice. He invites us by name. He stands arms outstretched, not only to welcome us in, but to show us that the only way in is through His death on the cross. We need to hear His voice, and accept this invitation, not just as a once off when we first became a Christian, but all day, every day, until the battle in this life is over.

'Listen, my son.'

MEMORY VERSE
'The fear of the Lord is the beginning of wisdom, and knowledge of the Holy One is understanding.' **Proverbs 9:10**

SUMMARY
Gary, listen my son. God invites you to come to Him on the basis of His undeserved kindness. He's inviting you to what you don't deserve. Never forget that. And you need to come to Him every single day by turning from the old you, and walking towards Him and walking in His ways.

GARY
Gary is finding his new faith a far greater challenge and fight than he ever imagined it would be. On the one hand he is experiencing God's grace and forgiveness and for the first time his life seems to be making sense to him. Yet he also finds himself going to war every day against temptation and sin and friends who are giving him a hard time for the choices he is making. He is very aware of just how weak and messed up he really is. He desperately needs others to help him and guide him to live a life that pleases Jesus.

There are so many different voices in Gary's life all screaming at him different things. His friends are telling him that he has gone soft and this church nonsense is a joke. The voices in his head are telling him it's too hard, he is not good enough, and that he will never be like these other Christians who seem to have their life together. His gambling buddies are on his case about getting back in the game. So many voices, but one voice above all will lead to life and contentment in this world. It is the voice of God revealed to us by the Holy Spirit through the Bible.

Although Gary is struggling to make sense of the Bible, he is really beginning to love to read it, as he is seeing that it is in the Bible we hear the voice of God.

How about you?

What voices are you listening to?

How are you being led by God who is speaking to us through the Bible?

9Marks

Building Healthy Churches

9Marks exists to equip church leaders with a biblical vision and practical resources for displaying God's glory to the nations through healthy churches.

To that end, we want to see churches characterised by these nine marks of health:

1   **Expositional Preaching**
2   **Biblical Theology**
3   **A Biblical Understanding of the Gospel**
4   **A Biblical Understanding of Conversion**
5   **A Biblical Understanding of Evangelism**
6   **Biblical Church Membership**
7   **Biblical Church Discipline**
8   **Biblical Discipleship**
9   **Biblical Church Leadership**

Find more titles at
www.9Marks.org

20schemes

Gospel Churches for Scotland's Poorest

20schemes exists to bring gospel hope to Scotland's poorest communities through the revitalisation and planting of healthy, gospel-preaching churches, ultimately led by a future generation of indigenous church leaders.

> *'If we are really going to see a turnaround in the lives of residents in our poorest communities, then we have to embrace a radical and long-term strategy which will bring gospel-hope to untold thousands.'*
>
> **MEZ MCCONNELL,** Ministry Director

We believe that building healthy churches in Scotland's poorest communities will bring true, sustainable, and long-term renewal to countless lives.

THE NEED IS URGENT

Learn more about our work and how to partner with us at:

20SCHEMES.COM
TWITTER.COM/20SCHEMES
FACEBOOK.COM/20SCHEMES
INSTAGRAM.COM/20SCHEMES